KS2 Success

Age 7-11

English

Laura Griffiths and Shelley Welsh

Test

Practice Papers

Contents

(pull-out section at the back of the book)

Introduction and instructions

How these tests will help your child

This book is made up of two complete sets of practice test papers. Each set contains similar test papers to those that your child will take at the end of Year 6 in English reading and English grammar, punctuation and spelling. They can be used any time throughout the year to provide practice for the Key Stage 2 tests.

The results of both sets of papers will provide a good idea of the strengths and weaknesses of your child.

Administering the tests

- Provide your child with a quiet environment where they can complete each test undisturbed.
- Provide your child with a pen or pencil, ruler and eraser.
- The amount of time given for each test varies, so remind your child at the start of each one how long they have and give them access to a clock or watch.
- You should only read the instructions out to your child, not the actual questions.
- Although handwriting is not assessed, remind your child that their answers should be clear.

English reading

- Each test is made up of three different texts and an answer booklet.
- Answers are worth 1, 2 or 3 marks, with a total number of 50 marks for each test.
- Your child will have **one hour** to read the texts in the reading booklet and answer questions in the answer booklet.
- Some questions are multiple choice, some are short answers where only a word or phrase is required, and others are longer and followed by several lines on which to write the answer.
- Encourage your child to look at the mark scheme after each question to help them know how much detail is required in their answer.

English grammar, punctuation and spelling

Paper 1: questions

- Contains 50 questions, with each answer worth 1 mark.
- Your child will have **45 minutes** to complete the test paper.
- Some questions are multiple choice and may require a tick in the box next to the answer. Some require a word or phrase to be underlined or circled while others have a line or box for the answer. Some questions ask for missing punctuation marks to be inserted.

Paper 2: spelling

- Contains 20 spellings, with each spelling worth 1 mark.
- Your child will have approximately **15 minutes** to complete the test paper.
- Using the spelling test administration guide on pages 101–102, read each spelling and allow your child time to fill it in on their spelling paper.

Marking the practice test papers

The answers and mark scheme have been provided to enable you to check how your child has performed. Fill in the marks that your child achieved for each part of the tests.

Please note: these tests are **only a guide** to the level or mark your child can achieve and cannot guarantee the same level is achieved during the Key Stage 2 tests.

English reading

	Set A	Set B
English reading paper	/50	/50

These scores roughly correspond with these levels: up to 20 = well below required level; 21–30 = below required level; 31–40 = meets required level; 41–50 = exceeds required level.

English grammar, punctuation and spelling

	Set A	Set B
Paper 1: questions	/50	/50
Paper 2: spelling	/20	/20
Total	/70	/70

These scores roughly correspond with these levels: up to 24 = well below required level; 25–43 = below required level; 44–53 = meets required level; 54–70 = exceeds required level.

When an area of weakness has been identified, it is useful to go over these, and similar types of questions, with your child. Sometimes your child will be familiar with the subject matter but might not understand what the question is asking. This will become apparent when talking to your child.

Shared marking and target setting

Engaging your child in the marking process will help them to develop a greater understanding of the tests and, more importantly, provide them with some ownership of their learning. They will be able to see more clearly how and why certain areas have been identified for them to target for improvement.

Top tips for your child

Don't make silly mistakes. Make sure you emphasise to your child the importance of reading the question. Easy marks can be picked up by just doing as the question asks.

Make answers clearly legible. If your child has made a mistake, encourage them to put a cross through it and write the correct answer clearly next to it. Try to encourage your child to use an eraser as little as possible.

Don't panic! These practice test papers, and indeed the Key Stage 2 tests, are meant to provide a guide to the level a child has attained. They are not the be-all and end-all, as children are assessed regularly throughout the school year. Explain to your child that there is no need to worry if they cannot do a question – tell them to go on to the next question and come back to the problematic question later if they have time.

Key Stage 2

English reading

Reading answer booklet

Time:

You have **one hour** to read the texts in the reading booklet (pages 75–83) and answer the questions in this answer booklet.

Maximum mark	Actual mark
50	....

First name	
Last name	

Date of birth	Day		Month		Year	

1 Where is the scene set?

_____
1 mark

2 Why is Alice very small?

_____
1 mark

3 Look at the opening conversation.

Find and **copy** the clause Alice says just before she sits down at the table.

_____
1 mark

4 Which character offered Alice a drink?

Tick **one**.

the Hare ☐

the Hatter ☐

the Narrator ☐

the Dormouse ☐

1 mark

5 Use the following line to answer question 5.

Alice: *Then it wasn't very civil of you to offer it!*

What does the word *civil* mean in this line?

Tick **one**.

polite ☐

angry ☐

old ☐

rude ☐

1 mark

6 Look at the Narrator's opening lines.

Identify **one** phrase that suggests Alice is correct in saying there is room for her to sit down.

_____

_____

1 mark

7 Explain why Alice says, *'it's very rude!'*.

_____

_____

1 mark

8 What stops the characters arguing?

_____

_____ 1 mark

9 At the end of the passage the Narrator says, '_The conversation drops_'.

What does the word _drops_ mean in this context?

_____ 1 mark

10 After reading the text, how would you describe the character Alice?

_____

_____ 1 mark

11 This text has been written as a play script.

Give **two** features of this genre that appear in the text.

1. _____

2. _____ 1 mark

12 Look at the title of the extract: *A Mad Tea Party*.

Explain fully why this is an appropriate title, referring to the text in your answer.

_____

_____

_____

1 mark

13 **Find** and **copy one** stage direction from the text.

_____

1 mark

14 What is a synonym for the word *riddle*?

Tick one.

solution ☐

puzzle ☐

sentence ☐

argument ☐

1 mark

15 Explain the role of the Narrator in the play script.

_____

_____

16 Look at the title of the extract: **_A Mad Tea Party_**.

Which of the following would be the most suitable replacement for this title?

Tick **one**.

An Ordinary Tea Party ☐

An Unusual Tea Party ☐

A Boring Tea Party ☐

A Quiet Tea Party ☐

17 What is the name of the largest island of the Isles of Scilly?

_____

1 mark

18 *The Isles of Scilly are made up of five inhabited and approximately 140 other islands.*

What does the word *inhabited* mean?

Tick one.

deserted ☐

far away ☐

people live there ☐

tropical ☐

1 mark

19 Look at the paragraph beginning: *To reach the Isles of Scilly from the mainland . . .*

Give **two** ways visitors can reach the islands.

1. _____

2. _____

1 mark

11

20 Read the advantages and disadvantages of the two methods of transport. Which would you recommend for the following visitors? Give reasons for your answers **using the information in the text**.

A day visitor with no luggage: _____

_____

_____

_____
1 mark

A family who are staying for a week who want to see dolphins swimming:

_____

_____

_____
1 mark

21 What does the word *common* mean in the sentence below?

There are many different types of birds on the islands, ranging from common birds such as sparrows, thrushes and gulls, to more unusual birds like puffins, cuckoos and wheatears.

_____

_____
1 mark

22 Would you like to visit the Isles of Scilly? Give **three** reasons for your view. Use the text to help you.

1. _____

2. _____

3. _____
1 mark

23 Compare how someone participating in and someone watching a gig race would be involved.

Participating: _____

_____

Watching: _____

_____

2 marks

24 This text was written to **inform** people about the Isles of Scilly.

Give **two** features of information writing that appear in the text.

- _____

- _____

2 marks

25 List **three** activities that the leaflet suggests for tourists to do when visiting the Isles of Scilly.

1. _____

2. _____

3. _____

1 mark

26 How do the locals usually travel around the islands? Give **two** modes of transport.

1. _____

2. _____

1 mark

27 In what format are you most likely to see this text?

Tick **one**.

a poster ☐

a travel leaflet ☐

a storybook ☐

a school magazine ☐

1 mark

28 When describing what tourists can see and do on the Isles of Scilly, the writer has deliberately chosen language that will have an effect on the reader.

Some of the words in the table below are underlined.

Explain the effect of these words in each sentence.

Language used	Explanation of the effect of the language
. . . *flock* to the island to race . . .	
. . . *waiting* to be explored . . .	
. . . *swirling golden* beaches . . .	

3 marks

29 What is the setting for the passage?

_____

1 mark

30 Why did Joseph say, *'It's the whole world, this place is'*?

Tick **one**.

He thinks it's the best place to be. ☐

He doesn't know life anywhere else. ☐

1 mark

31 *. . . Jim was looking up at the high walls that surrounded the workhouse, and at the bleak sky above it.*

Give **one** reason why the walls were high.

_____

1 mark

32 Look at the paragraph that starts *It was impossible to tell . . .*

Explain how in this paragraph Jim realises he's been in the workhouse for a year.

_____

_____

_____

_____

1 mark

33 *It was then that the little secret promise that had nestled inside him began to flutter into life like a wild thing.*

At this point in the story, what do you think Jim was thinking?
What was the *little secret promise*?

_____

_____

_____

1 mark

34 *The teacher hauled him off his stool . . .*

Which word below is a synonym for the word *hauled*?

Tick one.

poked ☐

pushed ☐

persuaded ☐

pulled ☐

1 mark

35 Why did Jim say he didn't mind when Mr Barrack was beating him?

_____

_____

1 mark

36 What reasons did Tip give for not going with Jim?

_____

_____
1 mark

37 *'A daft boy, you are,' said Tip.*

Do you think Tip was correct to say this to Jim? Give examples from the text to support your answer.

_____

_____
1 mark

38 Describe the relationship between the two main characters, Jim and Tip, throughout the extract. Give examples from the text to support your answer.

_____

_____

_____

_____

_____
2 marks

39 Why did Jim say, '*Seems like I was born here*'?

_____ 1 mark

40 Draw a line to match each event below to show the correct order from 1–6, as it appears in the extract.

Mr Sissons asked for big boys to help.	1
Jim asked Tip to run away with him.	2
Jim tried to remember what life outside the workhouse was like.	3
Tip shared his supper with Jim.	4
Mr Barrack gave Jim a beating.	5
Jim decided to climb over the wall and escape.	6

1 mark

41 Find and copy **two** words which suggest Mr Barrack was pleased he had caught Jim talking.

Mr Barrack sprang down from his chair, his eyes alight with anger and joy. 'You spoke!' he said to Jim, triumphant. 'It was you.'

_____

_____

1 mark

42 When describing Jim's feelings throughout the extract, the writer has deliberately chosen language that will have an effect on the reader.

Some of the words in the table below are underlined.

Explain the effect of these words in each sentence.

Language used	Explanation of the effect of the language
Jim's wild thoughts drummed inside him . . .	
. . . the beating inside him was like a wild bird now . . .	
. . . a shimmer of pain and thrumming wings.	

3 marks

SET
A

English
grammar,
punctuation
and spelling

PAPER 1

Key Stage 2

English grammar, punctuation and spelling

Paper 1: questions

Time:

You have **45 minutes** to complete this test paper.

Maximum mark	Actual mark
50	

First name	
Last name	

Date of birth	Day		Month		Year	

1 Tick the boxes where **determiners** have been used correctly.

Tick **two**.

an elephant ☐

an drum ☐

a octopus ☐

a superhero ☐

1 mark

2 Tick the word that means <u>to find out</u>.

Tick **one**.

choose ☐

discover ☐

invite ☐

repeat ☐

1 mark

3 Circle one verb in each underlined pair to complete the sentences using **Standard English**.

We **was / were** going to play outside on our bikes.

I **done / did** well in my maths test this morning.

1 mark

4   Add **inverted commas** to each direct speech below.

Wait for me! shouted Orla.

Ouch! My hand hurts.

Freddie whispered, Are you scared?

5   Circle the **verb** in the sentence below.

Olivia and Sandip were building sandcastles at the beach.

6   Which sentence shows the correct agreement between **subject** and **verb**?

Tick **one**.

The authors writed letters to the newspaper. ☐

The authors wrote letters to the newspaper. ☐

The authors write letter to the newspaper. ☐

The authors writes letters to the newspaper. ☐

7   Add the missing **full stops** and **capital letters** to the sentence below.

nottingham is located in the east midlands the river that runs

through nottingham is called the river trent

8   Circle the **conjunction** in the sentence below.

Since it was very cold outside, Sam decided to fasten his coat.

1 mark

9   Draw a line to match each **prefix** to the root word to make a new word.

dis		haul

mis		honest

over		understood

1 mark

10   Add an **apostrophe** in the correct places to show possession.

Emmas cat had five kittens last night.

The boys changing rooms were locked.

Jamies lunchbox was left overnight in his classroom.

1 mark

11   Rewrite the sentence adding **two dashes** in the correct places.

William Shakespeare a famous author wrote the play 'Macbeth'.

_____

_____

1 mark

12   Underline the **main clause** in the sentence below.

Although she is younger than me, my sister is much taller.

1 mark

13   The incomplete sentences below are instructions in a recipe.
Add **two adverbials of time** to make the two sentences correct.
Remember to use correct punctuation.

_____ check you have the correct ingredients.

_____ turn the oven on to 180 degrees.

1 mark

14   Choose **one** of the **question tags** below to complete the sentence.

haven't you	haven't we	didn't you

You've been learning about materials in science, _____?

1 mark

15   Use the **past progressive** form of the verbs in the box to complete
the sentence below.

to dance	to play

While the band _____, I _____ with
my friends.

1 mark

16   Tick the option that correctly introduces the **subordinate clause** in the sentence below.

The teacher was pleased with the children's work, _____ he gave them extra playtime!

Tick **one**.

despite ☐

therefore ☐

however ☐

finally ☐

1 mark

17   Insert a **comma** in the correct place in the sentence below.

Feeling confident the pianist played to a room full of people.

1 mark

18   Circle the **adjective** in the sentence below.

Mum carefully topped the pudding with some whipped cream.

1 mark

19 In the sentence below, what **word class** is the word they? Put a tick next to your answer.

I wish they would be quiet now!

Tick **one**.

adjective ☐

preposition ☐

verb ☐

pronoun ☐

1 mark

20 Which of the events below is the **most likely** to happen?

Tick **one**.

I will wash the car today. ☐

I should go to work. ☐

I might watch a film. ☐

I could play in the garden. ☐

1 mark

21 Draw a line to match the words to the correct sentence type.

Ouch!		question
How old are you?		statement
The music was very loud.		exclamation

1 mark

22 Circle the most suitable **pronoun** to complete the sentence below.

| he | his | it | me |

Zane ate his dinner and then _____ went outside to play.

23 Underline the **adverbial phrase** in the sentence below.

Later that evening, we said goodbye and began our journey home.

24 Add **three commas** in the correct places in the sentence below.

Mangoes kiwis apples pineapples and strawberries are all types

of fruit.

25 Write this sentence in the **past tense**.

We laugh at each other's funny jokes.

_____

26 Circle the **conjunction** in the sentence below.

I am allowed to watch television while eating my dinner.

27 Use the words below to complete the table.

| ancient | new | small | large | wealthy | poor |

	Synonym	Antonym
sad	unhappy	happy
rich		
big		
old		

1 mark

28 Insert the missing **punctuation** in the sentence below.

The skateboard park located behind the playground is to be used by children who are over eight

1 mark

29 Rewrite the sentence below putting **ellipses** in the correct places.

On your marks ready steady go!

_____

1 mark

30 Rewrite the sentence below in the **active** voice.

The ancient ruins were visited by the historians.

_____

1 mark

31 Change the **nouns** to **verbs**.

Noun	Verb
simplification	to
calculation	to
magnification	to

1 mark

32 Circle the **preposition** in the sentence below.

The girl walked up the stairs.

1 mark

33 Rewrite the sentence below adding a **subordinate clause**.
Remember to use the correct punctuation.

The farmer went into his field.

_____

_____

_____

1 mark

34 Write out the words from the boxes below to make **one** sentence.
You can use the boxes in any order.
Remember to punctuate your answer correctly.

came to visit us	at Christmas
who lives in France	My uncle

_____

_____

1 mark

35 Underline the **relative clause** in the sentence below.

The old lady who was shouting at her neighbour was feeling angry.

1 mark

36 Write a suitable question to fit the answer below.
Remember to use the correct punctuation.

Question _____

Answer   He takes the bus.

1 mark

37 Circle the **two** words that show a **command** in the sentences below.

Put the flour and the butter in the bowl. Mix them together carefully.

1 mark

38 Write a **pronoun** in the space to make the sentence correct.

The boy ran up the school drive. _____ was late again!

1 mark

39 Complete the sentence below with a **contraction** that makes sense.

Why _____ you find your homework?

1 mark

40 Choose the correct form of the **past tense** of the verbs below to show a **continuous action**.

to dance

When I _____ in the show I

to smile

_____ all the time.

41 Add **inverted commas** to punctuate the speech below.

What time does the train leave the station? Mary asked the guard.

Three minutes past ten, the guard answered.

42 Where should a **question mark** be added to make the sentence below correct?

Tick **one**.

"Where are you going" the bus driver asked.

43 Use the **co-ordinating conjunctions** in the box to correctly complete the sentence below.
Use each conjunction **once**.

| or | but | and |

The books _____ DVDs need returning to the library on

Monday _____ Tuesday _____ remember

it is closed each day for lunch.

44 Rewrite the sentence below so that it starts with a **subordinate clause**. Remember to use a **comma** in the correct place.

I read a book while I was waiting to see the doctor.

_____

1 mark

45 Which of the sentences uses **dashes** correctly?

Tick **one**.

The cat – fast asleep – on the rug – was keeping warm by the fire. ☐

The cat – fast asleep on the rug – was keeping warm by the fire. ☐

The cat fast asleep, on the rug – was keeping warm – by the fire. ☐

The cat – fast asleep on the rug, – was keeping warm by the fire. ☐

1 mark

46 Underline the **fronted adverbial** in the sentence below.

With his sports kit on, Tom was ready for the game.

1 mark

47 Use the **subjunctive mood** to complete the sentence below so that it becomes more **formal**.

If the bus _____ late again, the children would be cross.

1 mark

48 Complete the table below by adding a **suffix** to each noun to make an **adjective**.

Noun	Adjective
child	
courage	
despair	
hope	
caution	

1 mark

49 What does the root <u>circ</u> mean in the word family below?

circumference   **circle**   **circumnavigate**

Tick **one**.

around   ☐

behind   ☐

above   ☐

below   ☐

1 mark

50 Circle one **verb** in each underlined pair to complete the sentences using **Standard English**.

I **went / goes** swimming at the weekend.

My friends Joe and Stella **was / were** there too.

1 mark

Key Stage 2

English grammar, punctuation and spelling

Paper 2: spelling

You will need to ask someone to read the instructions and sentences to you. These can be found on page 101.

Time:

You have approximately **15 minutes** to complete this test paper.

Maximum mark	Actual mark
20	

First name	
Last name	

Date of birth	Day		Month		Year	

Spelling

1 Jai hurt his _____ playing tennis with his friends.

2 The _____ forecast for today is mostly sunny and warm.

3 Our _____ little kitten had scratched the carpet.

4 Mangoes, pineapples, kiwis and oranges are all types of _____.

5 We are going on a _____ hunt tomorrow.

6 The new clothes didn't fit so I need to _____ them to the shop.

7 My ambition is to play football for my _____.

8 The _____ was extremely busy this afternoon.

9 At break time, we play with the outdoor _____.

10 The _____ water boils at is 100 degrees Celsius.

11 The doctor said the rash was highly _____.

12 Sam won a _____ he entered at school.

13 Jemima was an _____ height for her age.

14 Our family eats _____ for breakfast.

15 The actress was very _____ on the stage.

16 The flowers in the bathroom are _____.

17 The weather is very _____ today.

18 There is a _____ coming from the large window.

19 The building must be evacuated _____ if the fire alarm rings.

20 The _____ members all attended a meeting at the school last night.

Key Stage 2

English reading

Reading answer booklet

Time:

You have **one hour** to read the texts in the reading booklet (pages 85–92) and answer the questions in this answer booklet.

Maximum mark	Actual mark
50	

First name	
Last name	

Date of birth	Day		Month		Year	

1 Look at the sentence.

It felt soft and warm and slightly furry, like the skin of a baby mouse.

The sentence contains:

Tick **one**.

a metaphor ☐

a simile ☐

personification ☐

alliteration ☐

1 mark

2 *James stopped and stared at the speakers, his face white with horror. He started to stand up, but his knees were shaking so much he had to sit down again on the floor.*

Write how James is feeling.

_____

1 mark

3 *The creatures, some sitting on chairs, others reclining on a sofa, were all watching him intently.*

Which word is the correct synonym of *intently*?

Tick one.

casually ☐

closely ☐

quickly ☐

strangely ☐

1 mark

4 Draw a line to match each creature to the description James gives when he **first** meets them.

Old-Green-Grasshopper		nine black spots on her scarlet shell
Spider		enormous
Silkworm		as large as a large dog
Ladybird		thick and white

1 mark

5 *He glanced behind him, thinking he could bolt back into the tunnel . . .*

What does the word *bolt* mean in this sentence?

_____

1 mark

6 What reason does the Ladybird give for James looking *'...as though he's going to faint any second'*?

_____

_____
1 mark

7 Explain as fully as you can what the Ladybird means when she tells James, *'You are one of us now, didn't you know that?'*

_____

_____
1 mark

8 Put a tick in the correct box to show whether each of the following statements is **true** or **false**.

	True	False
A fence surrounded the peach.		
The tunnel was dry and cold.		
James bumped his head on the stone in the middle of the peach.		
James couldn't stand up because the peach wasn't big enough.		
The creatures were at least the same size as James.		

1 mark

9 What **effect** is the author trying to create in the sentence below?

Four pairs of round black glassy eyes were all fixed upon James.

_____

_____

_____

_____

2 marks

10 Which words does the author use to create a magical setting in the first paragraph?

Use examples from the text below.

The garden lay soft and silver in the moonlight. The grass was wet with dew and a million dewdrops were sparkling and twinkling like diamonds around his feet. And now suddenly, the whole place, the whole garden seemed to be alive with magic.

_____

_____

_____

2 marks

11 Explain why this statement by the Centipede is funny.

And meanwhile I wish you'd come over here and give me a hand with these boots. It takes me hours to get them all off by myself.

_____

_____

_____

1 mark

12 Which **two** parts of his body did James put into the peach first?

1. _____

2. _____   1 mark

13 *The floor was soggy under his knees.*

What does the word *soggy* mean in this sentence?

_____   1 mark

14 When James realised that the hole in the peach was a tunnel, how did he feel?

_____   1 mark

15 When James first entered the room at the centre of the peach, which **two** characters were seated next to the Spider?

1. _____

2. _____   1 mark

16 What type of writing is featured in this account?

Tick **one**.

diary ☐

autobiography ☐

biography ☐

story ☐

1 mark

17 Where was Floella born?

_____

1 mark

18 What does the word *challenging* mean in the sentence below?

Initially she found it very different to her life in Trinidad and growing up in two cultures was challenging.

_____

_____

1 mark

19 Floella Benjamin's family are special to her.

Find and **copy two** sentences that infer Floella had a good relationship with her parents.

Mum: _____

_____

Dad: _____

_____

2 marks

20 What is the name of Floella's autobiography?

_____

1 mark

21 What was the name of the drama in which Floella made her TV debut?

_____

1 mark

22 Find the year when each of the events below happened in Floella Benjamin's life. Write the answers in the grid below.

Event	Date
Born	
Came to England	
Made her TV debut	
Started her own television production company	
Wrote *Coming to England*	
Trekked the Great Wall of China	

2 marks

23 In what order is the text written?

Tick **one**.

importance ☐

no particular order ☐

chronological ☐

1 mark

24 For which charity does Floella raise money by running the London Marathon?

Tick **one**.

Sickle Cell Society ☐

Action for Children ☐

Barnardo's ☐

NSPCC ☐

1 mark

25 This text was written to **inform** people about the life of Floella Benjamin.

Give **two** features of information writing that appear in the text.

1. _____

2. _____

1 mark

26 Summarise **three** ways we know that Floella has helped children's charities.

1. _____

_____

2. _____

_____

3. _____

_____

2 marks

27 Put a tick in the correct box to show whether each of the following statements about Floella is **fact** or **opinion**.

	Fact	Opinion
She worked in a bank.		
She loved her job on *Play School*.		
She presented *Play School* for 12 years.		
She has completed ten London Marathons.		
She is a keen runner.		

1 mark

28 Explain how Floella Benjamin's childhood influenced her to help young people across the world.

_____

_____

_____

2 marks

29 What happens when someone goes to investigate a crime Macavity has committed?

_____

1 mark

30 Look at the third verse.

This verse tells readers more information about Macavity's

Tick **one**.

friends.   ☐

personality.   ☐

hobbies.   ☐

appearance.   ☐

1 mark

31 What does the word *neglect* mean in the third verse?

_____

_____

1 mark

32 Look at the first line of the poem.

Macavity's a Mystery Cat:

Explain why the poet describes Macavity as a *Mystery Cat*.

_____

_____

1 mark

33 Why do you think the poet uses **repetition** of the phrase '*Macavity's not there*'?

_____

_____

_____

1 mark

34 *He always has an alibi, and one or two to spare:*

Explain what this line means.

_____

_____

1 mark

35 What type of poem is *Macavity*?

Tick one.

limerick ☐

narrative ☐

Haiku ☐

sonnet ☐

1 mark

36 Describe the poet's use of **rhyme** throughout the poem.

_____

_____

_____ 1 mark

37 _MACAVITY WASN'T THERE!_

In the final verse, why do you think the poet changed the repetition and used capital letters?

_____

_____

_____ 1 mark

38 Put a tick in the correct box to show whether each of the following statements is **fact** or **opinion**.

	Fact	Opinion
It is fun watching Macavity cause trouble.		
Macavity's a ginger cat.		
His coat is dusty.		
Macavity has no-one to care for him.		

1 mark

39 **Find** and **copy** a simile from verse three.

_____

1 mark

40 In verse five, **find** and **copy one** word which means the same as _stolen_.

_____

1 mark

41 In the final verse, explain what the poet means by '_Just controls their operations: the Napoleon of Crime!_'

_____

_____

1 mark

42 Summarise **three** main ideas the poet implies about Macavity's characteristics throughout the poem.

1. _____

_____

2. _____

_____

3. _____

_____

3 marks

SET
B

English
grammar,
punctuation
and spelling

PAPER 1

Key Stage 2

English grammar, punctuation and spelling

Paper 1: questions

Time:

You have **45 minutes** to complete this test paper.

Maximum mark	Actual mark
50	

First name	
Last name	

Date of birth	Day		Month		Year	

1 Circle **all** the **adjectives** in the sentence below.

The creepy shadows darted quickly past the wooden fence, along the hidden path and into the gloomy garage.

1 mark

2 Which word completes the sentence below?

You cannot go on the field today _____ it is too muddy.

Tick **one**.

however ☐

although ☐

because ☐

and ☐

1 mark

3 Circle one verb in each underlined pair to complete the sentence using **Standard English**.

I **did / done** a detailed piece of writing.

They **has / have** been playing outside.

1 mark

4 Rewrite the sentences below adding **apostrophes** in the correct place to mark **possession**.

The dogs tail was wagging.

_____

The boys coats were on the floor.

_____

The womens changing rooms were busy.

_____ 1 mark

5 Rewrite the sentence below so that it begins with the **adverbial**. Use only the same words and remember to punctuate your answer correctly.

Kenzie blew out the candles after the singing.

_____

_____ 1 mark

6 Add an adjective before each noun to make an **expanded noun phrase**.

The _____ skateboard park.

The _____ holiday. 1 mark

7 Write the name of the punctuation circled in the sentence below.

Then, all of a sudden, lightning struck (. . .) boom!

_____

1 mark

8 Insert a **semi-colon** in the most appropriate place in the sentence below.

Grace bought a bouncy ball she played with it in the garden.

1 mark

9 Tick one box in each row to show if the underlined noun is a **proper noun** or a **common noun**.

Sentence	Proper noun	Common noun
My birthday is in <u>January</u>.		
The <u>bees</u> landed on the flower.		
The car towed the <u>caravan</u>.		
His brother's name is <u>Andrew</u>.		

1 mark

10 Write a suitable **modal verb** in the sentence below.

They really _____ take more care.

1 mark

11 Change the verb below into a **noun**.

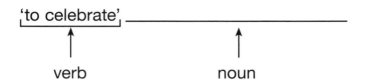

'to celebrate' _____

　　　　↑　　　　　　　　　↑
　　　verb　　　　　　　noun

12 Draw a line to show whether each sentence is written in the **active** or **passive voice**.

| Rosie climbed the stairs. |

| The stairs were climbed by Rosie. |

| passive |

| active |

13 Circle the **conjunction** in the sentence below.

The girls were tired but it was too early to go to bed.

14 Circle the words in the sentence below that make it a **question**.

"You were expecting this letter today, weren't you?"

15 Underline the **relative clause** in the sentence below.

The ice cream van that is in the car park is very popular today.

16 Use each **preposition** from the box to complete the sentences below.

under	in	along

She walked _____ the canal path.

The dog hid _____ the table.

I was lost _____ the maze.

1 mark

17 Which sentence contains **two verbs**?

Tick **one**.

I ran home very quickly. ☐

The teacher read a very long story. ☐

The little boy watched TV and ate a sandwich. ☐

The spider crawled underneath the doormat. ☐

1 mark

18 Circle **all** the **determiners** in the sentence below.

An alligator is a large reptile.

1 mark

19 Complete the sentence using suitable **pronouns**.

Rosie's homework was too hard for _____ and

_____ felt sad that _____

couldn't do it.

1 mark

20 Which of the events in the sentences below is the **most** likely to happen?

Tick **one**.

We might go to the cinema tonight. ☐

He will go to school tomorrow. ☐

They could go camping at the weekend. ☐

I can go to your party tomorrow. ☐

1 mark

21 Write a suitable **question tag** at the end of the statements below.

It's a nice day today, _____

You like reading, _____

1 mark

22 Insert a set of **brackets** so that the sentence below is punctuated correctly.

Mrs Jones the Year 5 teacher played the piano in school today.

1 mark

23 Add a **subordinate clause** to the main clause below.

_____, I went

to the park.

1 mark

24 Insert a **comma** in the correct place in the sentence below.

Hanging upside down the bat made loud noises as the night sky grew darker.

1 mark

25 Complete the table by inserting a **synonym** and an **antonym**.

Word	Synonym	Antonym
stiff		
angry		

1 mark

26 Circle the correct form of the underlined **verb** in each sentence.

The tree **sway / sways** gently in the breeze.

The goats **have / has** two horns each.

The children **are / is** too noisy!

1 mark

27 To make a pop-up book, Louis needs three pieces of equipment: scissors, card and glue.
Rewrite this sentence as an instruction using a **colon** and **bullet points**.

To make a pop-up book you will need three things

_____

_____

_____

1 mark

28 Choose a suitable **prefix** for the following verbs:

_____ cover

_____ place

_____ allow

1 mark

29 Write **two conjunctions** to complete the sentence below.

I like drawing _____ painting

_____ my sister prefers writing.

1 mark

30 Rewrite the sentence below so that it begins with an **adverbial**.
Remember to punctuate your sentence correctly.

We went to the cinema after tea.

_____

1 mark

31 Rewrite the sentence below using **direct speech**.
Remember to punctuate your sentence correctly.

Mrs Shepherd told her class there will be an important visitor in assembly.

_____

_____

1 mark

32   Put **commas** in the correct places to separate items in the list below.

The milkman delivers fresh produce on a Monday Tuesday Thursday and Saturday.

33   Add the pronouns **I** and **me** to the sentences below to make them correct.

Noah and _____ went for a walk in the woods.

Our parents told my sister and _____ to hurry up.

34   Circle the **preposition** in the sentence.

The cat slept in the warm, cosy basket.

35   Which of the sentences below uses the **semi-colon** correctly?

Tick **one**.

Ella played the piano; Alex played the flute. ☐

Ella played; the piano Alex played; the flute. ☐

Ella played; the piano; Alex played the flute. ☐

Ella; played the piano Alex; played the flute. ☐

36 Put a tick in each row to show if the words on the left are **adverbs of time** or **place**.

Adverb	Time (when)	Place (where)
frequently		
regularly		
often		
in the middle of		

1 mark

37 Underline the **relative clause** in the sentence below.

Brighton, which is a seaside town, is located on the south coast of England.

1 mark

38 Add the words from the boxes below to this sentence starter to make **one** sentence.
Remember to punctuate your answer correctly.

| when she got a puppy for her birthday | | was thrilled |

| who loves dogs | | Hayley |

My best friend _____

_____

1 mark

39 Write this sentence as **direct speech** using **inverted commas**.

I told my brother it was my turn next.

_____

1 mark

40 Contract these words using an **apostrophe**.

should have _____

they will _____

he is _____

41 Insert the correct punctuation into this sentence.
The first one has been done for you.

D
~~d~~uring his stay on the farm jon saw some ducks a herd of goats

and a huge pink pig

42 Put a tick in each row to show whether each **explanation** is **true** or **false**.

Explanation	True	False
A <u>request</u> is to ask for something.		
An <u>indulgent</u> is an invitation.		
A <u>container</u> is used to put things in.		
A <u>bleak</u> morning is a dismal one.		

43 Write the **basic form** of each verb.

laughs, laughed = to _____

walks, walked = to _____

flies, flew = to _____

grows, grew = to _____

44 Rewrite the sentence below using **Standard English**.

I've not got none.

_____

1 mark

45 Complete the table below by adding a **suffix** to each verb to make a **noun**.

Verb	Noun
agree	
refer	
form	
assist	

1 mark

46 What does the root word <u>fin</u> mean in the word family below?

finite	infinity	finish

Tick one.

beginning ☐

distant ☐

end ☐

nearby ☐

1 mark

47 Underline the **modal verb** in the sentence below.

We should have stayed late at school tonight.

1 mark

48 Rewrite the sentence below, changing it to the **past progressive tense**.

I eat all my dinner.

_____

1 mark

49 The sentence below has an **apostrophe** missing.
Rewrite the sentence and **explain** why the apostrophe is needed.

Annies mum worked at the school library.

_____

_____

_____

1 mark

50 Which word completes the sentence so that it uses the **subjunctive mood**?

The Head Teacher said, "If there _____ to be a fire, students should exit through the rear doors."

Tick **one**.

was	☐
were	☐
had	☐
going	☐

1 mark

SET
B

English
grammar,
punctuation
and spelling

PAPER 2

Key Stage 2

English grammar, punctuation and spelling

Paper 2: spelling

You will need to ask someone to read the instructions and sentences to you. These can be found on pages 101–102.

Time:

You have approximately **15 minutes** to complete this test paper.

Maximum mark	Actual mark
20	

First name	
Last name	

Date of birth	Day		Month		Year	

Spelling

1 The _____ of Majorca is close to Spain.

2 The chocolate cake was _____.

3 _____ can be mashed, chipped, boiled or baked.

4 A _____ should never be broken!

5 My _____ sport is cricket.

6 The _____ of the luggage is less than 15 kilograms.

7 _____ teachers have told me I have a talent for drawing.

8 The kittens are _____.

9 Playing football for the school team is a great _____.

10 All the _____ information should be underlined.

11 I am trying to _____ my mum to buy me some new boots.

12 My _____ feels full after lunch.

13 Mata listened to the story with _____.

14 The first time we met was a little _____.

15 Ned's _____ was the fastest.

16 The whole family is in _____ for our pet.

17 Because of the roadworks, the traffic was _____.

18 Coffee and fizzy drinks usually contain _____.

19 The gymnasts _____ their weight across the bars.

20 We do not mind what type of _____ we stay in on holiday.

Contents

English reading booklets

Reading booklet

Contents

A Mad Tea Party

Alice has just drunk a magic potion, which has made her very small. It enables her to enter Wonderland, where nothing is ever quite as it seems!

The scene begins in the garden. There is a table under a tree in front of a house. The March Hare and the Hatter are having tea at the table. A dormouse sits between them.

Narrator: The March Hare and the Mad Hatter are having tea, all squashed at one end of a very large table.

Alice: Hello, mind if I join you all?

Hare, Hatter, Dormouse: No room! No room!

Alice: What are you talking about, there's plenty of room.

Alice sits down.

Hare: Have some wine.

Alice: *(looking around the table)* I don't see any wine.

Hare: There isn't any.

Alice: *(in an angry voice)* Then it wasn't very civil of you to offer it!

Hare: It wasn't very civil of you to sit down without being invited.

Alice: I didn't know it was your table, it's laid for many more than three.

Hatter: *(looking up and down at Alice)* Your hair wants cutting.

Alice: You should learn not to make personal remarks. It's very rude!

Narrator: The characters continue arguing until the Hatter opens his eyes very wide and begins talking in riddles.

Hatter: Why is a raven like a writing desk?

Alice: I believe I can guess that.

Hare: Do you mean you think you can find the answer for it?

Alice: Exactly so.

Hare: Then you should say what you mean.

Alice: I do. At least, I mean what I say – that's the same thing you know.

Hatter: Not the same thing a bit! Why, you might just as well say that I like what I get is the same as I get what I like.

Dormouse: *(talking in a sleepy way)* I breathe when I sleep is the same thing as I sleep when I breathe!

Hatter: It is the same thing with you!

Narrator: The conversation drops, and the party sits silently for a minute.

(The Hatter takes his watch out of his pocket and looks at it uneasily; he shakes it and holds it to his ear. He then dips it in his cup of tea and looks at it again.)

The Isles of Scilly

Location

The Isles of Scilly are a group of islands located 45 km (28 miles) off the coast of the Cornish peninsula.

The Islands

The Isles of Scilly are made up of five inhabited and approximately 140 other islands. The largest of the islands is called St Mary's, with Tresco, St Martin's, St Agnes and Bryher being the others.

The main settlement on St Mary's is Hugh Town. This is a very small town with only a few shops, banks, restaurants, hotels and pubs. The population of Hugh Town is just over 1000.

Travel

Because the Isles of Scilly are so small, very few people own cars. Locals usually walk or ride bicycles. Public transport is a boat service between the islands.

To reach the Isles of Scilly from the mainland, visitors need to travel on either a small aeroplane (Skybus) or a passenger ferry (*The Scillonian*). These methods of transport are both an amazing experience for travellers to the islands and the table below lists the advantages and disadvantages of each.

	Skybus	**The Scillonian**
Advantages	Travel to and from three different mainland airports	Cafés serving hot and cold food on board
	Bird's-eye views of the islands	Often see dolphins, sea birds and basking sharks
	Quick	Seaside views
	Small and personal	Cheap
Disadvantages	Limited luggage allowed	Often rough seas and passengers may suffer motion sickness
	More expensive	Longer journey
	Flights can be cancelled because of high winds	

Weather

The Isles of Scilly have a unique climate, with the mildest and warmest temperatures in the United Kingdom. The average annual temperature is 11.8 °C (53.2 °F) in comparison to London, where it is 11.6 °C (52.9 °F).

The winters in Scilly are relatively warm and the islands very rarely get frosts or snow. They are however windy, due to the full force of the wind off the Atlantic Ocean.

Plants and Animals

The warm, humid climate of the Isles of Scilly allows a variety of rare plants and flowers to grow, which are not seen in other parts of the United Kingdom.

Some people describe the Scilly Islands as 'a large natural greenhouse'. Even in winter, there are hundreds of different plants in bloom.

Month	Jan	Feb	Mar	Apr	May	Jun	Jul	Aug	Sept	Oct	Nov	Dec
Average temp. °C (°F)	8.0 (46.4)	7.9 (46.2)	8.8 (47.8)	9.8 (49.6)	12.0 (53.5)	14.5 (58.1)	16.5 (61.7)	16.9 (62.5)	15.5 (59.8)	12.7 (54.8)	10.3 (50.6)	8.7 (47.6)

Because of the warm temperatures, many birds migrate to Scilly. Some birds stop off on their way across the Atlantic Ocean, while others stay on the islands. There are many different types of birds on the islands, ranging from common birds such as sparrows, thrushes and gulls, to more unusual birds like puffins, cuckoos and wheatears.

Tourism

The Isles of Scilly rely on tourism. The majority of shops, restaurants, bars and cafés earn money from visitors during the summer season. People travel to Scilly for many reasons. Quite often there are visitors who come on walking holidays, bird-watching trips and to relax on one of the quiet beaches.

Holidaymakers can choose accommodation suitable for their stay. The main islands have a choice of hotels, bed and breakfasts, self-catering cottages and camping facilities.

Activities

Many people choose to participate in water sports, including sailing, kayaking, boating and fishing.

The islands are famous for their clear waters, which also make snorkelling and diving popular activities.

'Gig racing' is the main sport on the Isles of Scilly. Gigs are traditional working boats, which six or seven people sit inside and row. Many islanders take part in gig practices and races throughout the season.

People watch the races and cheer on the gigs from passenger boats that follow the race or they sometimes watch the finish from the quay on St Mary's. The Isles of Scilly host an annual gig championship; thousands of rowers from as far away as Holland flock to the island to race at this event.

Historic Sites

The Isles of Scilly have many historic landmarks waiting to be explored, including castles, churches, lighthouses and ruins. There are art galleries and exhibitions, museums and often concerts to attend.

Probably the most impressive feature of the Isles of Scilly is its natural beauty; the swirling golden beaches, sand dunes, rocky coastlines and scenic views are well worth a visit.

Street Child

'Joseph,' Jim asked the bent man one day out in the yard. 'How long have you been here?'

'Been here?' Joseph swung his head round and peered up at Jim. 'Seems like I was born here. Don't know nothing else, son. And I don't know all of this place neither.' He leaned against Jim so he could swing his head up to look at the long, high building with its rows of barred windows. 'I've not been in the room where the women go, though long ago I must have been in the baby-room, I suppose, with my ma. I've been in the infirmary wards. But there's all kinds of little twisty corridors and attics and places I've never been in Jim, and I don't want to, neither. It's the whole world, this place is.' He spread out his hands. 'Whole world.'

'It ain't, Joseph,' Jim told him. 'There's no shops here, and no carriages. And no trees.' He closed his eyes, forcing himself to try and remember what it was like outside. 'And there's no river. There's a great big river outside here.'

'Is there now?' said Joseph. 'I should like to see that river. Though to tell you the truth, Jim, I don't know what a river is. Tell you something.' He put his arm over Jim's shoulder to draw his ear closer to his own mouth. 'I don't want to die in here. If someone will let me know what day I'm going to die, I'll be grateful. I'll climb over that wall first.' He dropped his head down again and stared at his boots, whistling softly. 'Yes. That's what I'll do.'

Tip spluttered and nudged Jim, but Jim was looking up at the high walls that surrounded the workhouse, and at the bleak sky above it.

'How long have I been here, Tip?' he asked.

'How should I know?' Tip hugged his arms round himself. 'Keep moving, Jim. It's cold.'

It was impossible to tell one day from the next. They were all the same. School, sack-making, bed. The only thing that changed was the sky. Jim had seen the grey of snow clouds turning into the soft rain clouds of spring. He'd felt summer scorching him in his heavy, itchy clothes. And now the sky was steely grey again. The pump had long beards of ice on its handle.

'I've been here a year,' Jim said. It was then that the little secret promise that had nestled inside him began to flutter into life like a wild thing.

'I've got to skip off,' he let the mad thought rise up in him.

'If I don't, I'll be like Joseph. One day I won't remember whether I was born here or not. I won't know anywhere but here.'

During lessons that day, the old schoolmaster's voice droned on in the dim schoolroom. The boys coughed and shuffled in their benches, hunching themselves against the cold. Jim's wild thoughts drummed inside him, so loud that he imagined everyone would hear them. He leaned over to Tip and whispered in his ear, 'Tip, I'm going to run away today. Come with me?' Tip sheered round, and put his hand to his mouth. Mr Barrack sprang down from his chair, his eyes alight with anger and joy.

'You spoke!' he said to Jim, triumphant. 'It was you.'

Tip closed his eyes and held out his hand, but Jim stood up. He didn't mind. He didn't mind anything any more. The teacher hauled him off his stool and swung his rope round. It hummed as it sliced through the air.

'I don't mind,' Jim tried to explain, but this made Mr Barrack angrier than ever. At last he had caught Jim out, and he was beating him now for every time he had tried and failed. He pulled a greasy handkerchief out of his pocket and wound it round Jim's head, tying it tight under his chin.

'Just in case you feels like hollering,' he said. All the other boys stared in front of them. The rope stung Jim again and again and the beating inside him was like a wild bird now, throbbing in his limbs and in his stomach, in his chest and in his head, so wild and loud that he felt it would lift him up and carry him away.

When the schoolmaster had finished with him he flung him like a bundle of rags across the desk. Jim lay in a shimmer of pain and thrumming wings. He wanted to sleep. The bell rang and the boys shuffled out. Jim felt Tip's hand on his shoulder. He flinched away.

'That's what they do to the boys who skip off, Jim,' Tip whispered. 'They thrash 'em like that every day until they are good.'

Jim felt the wild thing fluttering again. 'Only if they catch them.'

'They always catch 'em. Bobbies catch 'em and bring 'em in, and they get thrashed and thrashed.'

Jim struggled to sit up. The stinging rolled down his body. 'Won't you come with me?'

'I daresn't. Honest, I daresn't. Don't go, Jim.'

Jim looked up at the great archways of the schoolroom. He knew the words off by heart. *God is good. God is holy. God is just. God is love.*

'I've got to,' he said. 'And I'm going tonight, Tip.'

Jim knew that he would have to make his break before old Marion did her rounds for the night. He had no idea how he was going to do it. At suppertime he stuffed his cheese in his pocket, and Tip passed his own share along to him.

At the end of the meal, Mr Sissons stood up on his dais. All the shuffling and whispering stopped. He moved his body slowly round, which was his way of fixing his eyes on everyone, freezing them like statues.

'I'm looking for some big boys,' he said. 'To help with the carpet-beaters.' He waited in silence, but nobody moved.

'Just as I would expect. A rush to help, when there is sickness in the wards,' A cold sigh seemed to ripple through the room. Mr Sissons laughed into it in his dry, hissing way. 'It might be cholera, my dears. That's what I hear. I've two thousand mouths to feed here, and someone has to earn the money, cholera or not. Somebody has to buy the medicines. Somebody has to pay for the burials.' He moved his body round in its slow, watchful circle again. 'Plenty of big strong boys here, eating every crumb I give them and never a word of thanks.' He stepped down from his dais and

walked along the rows, cuffing boys on the back of their heads as he passed them. 'I want you all up in the women's wards straight after supper, and you don't come down again till all the carpets are done.'

'What's carpets?' asked Jim.

'Dunno,' Tip whispered, 'they come from the rich houses, and the women here beat 'em, and then they send them home.'

'I'm going with them,' Jim said suddenly, standing up as soon as the older boys did.

'A daft boy, you are,' said Tip. 'He asked for big boys.'

'You coming or not?' Jim darted off after the big boys and Tip ran after him.

Reading booklet

Contents

James and the Giant Peach

The garden lay soft and silver in the moonlight. The grass was wet with dew and a million dewdrops were sparkling and twinkling like diamonds around his feet. And now suddenly, the whole place, the whole garden seemed to be *alive* with magic.

Almost without knowing what he was doing, as though drawn by some powerful magnet, James Henry Trotter started walking slowly towards the giant peach. He climbed over the fence that surrounded it, and stood directly beneath it, staring up at its great bulging sides. He put out a hand and touched it gently with the tip of one finger. It felt soft and warm and slightly furry, like the skin of a baby mouse. He moved a step closer and rubbed his cheek lightly against the soft skin. And then suddenly, while he was doing this, he happened to notice that right beside him and below him, close to the ground, there was a hole in the side of the peach.

It was quite a large hole, the sort of thing an animal about the size of a fox might have made.

James knelt down in front of it and poked his head and shoulders inside.

He crawled in.

He kept on crawling.

This isn't just a hole, he thought excitedly. It's a tunnel!

The tunnel was damp and murky, and all around him there was the curious bittersweet smell of fresh peach. The floor was soggy under his knees, the walls were wet and sticky, and peach juice was dripping from the ceiling. James opened his mouth and caught some of it on his tongue. It tasted delicious.

He was crawling uphill now, as though the tunnel were leading straight towards the very centre of the gigantic fruit. Every few seconds he paused and took a bite out of the wall. The peach flesh was sweet and juicy, and marvellously refreshing.

He crawled on for several more yards, and then suddenly – bang – the top of his head

bumped into something extremely hard blocking his way. He glanced up.
In front of him there was a solid wall that seemed at first as though it were
made of wood. He touched it with his fingers. It certainly felt like wood,
except that it was very jagged and full of deep grooves.

'Good heavens!' he said. 'I know what this is! I've come to the stone in
the middle of the peach!'

Then he noticed that there was a small door cut into the face of the
peach stone. He gave a push. It swung open. He crawled through it, and before he had time to
glance up and see where he was, he heard a voice saying, 'Look who's here!' And another one
said, 'We've been waiting for you!'

James stopped and stared at the speakers, his face white with horror.

He started to stand up, but his knees were shaking so much he had to sit down again on the
floor. He glanced behind him, thinking he could bolt back into the tunnel the way he had come,
but the doorway had disappeared. There was now only a solid brown wall behind him.

James's large frightened eyes travelled slowly around the room.

The creatures, some sitting on chairs, others reclining on a sofa, were all watching him
intently.

Creatures?

Or were they insects?

An insect is usually something rather small, is it not? A grasshopper, for example, is an insect.

So what would you call it if you saw a grasshopper as large as a dog? As large as a *large*
dog. You could hardly call *that* an insect, could you?

There was an Old-Green-Grasshopper as large as a large dog sitting on a stool directly
across the room from James now.

And next to the Old-Green-Grasshopper, there was an enormous Spider.

And next to the Spider, there was a giant Ladybird with nine black spots on her scarlet shell.

Each of these three was squatting upon a magnificent chair.

On a sofa near by, reclining comfortably in curled-up positions, there was a Centipede and
an Earthworm.

On the floor over in the far corner, there was something thick and white that looked as though
it might be a Silkworm. But it was sleeping soundly and nobody was paying any attention to it.

Every one of these creatures was at least as big as James himself, and in the strange greenish light that shone down from somewhere in the ceiling, they were absolutely terrifying to behold.

'I'm hungry!' the Spider announced suddenly, staring hard at James.

'*I'm* famished!' the Old-Green-Grasshopper said.

'So am *I*!' the Ladybird cried.

The Centipede sat up a little straighter on the sofa. '*Everyone's* famished!' he said. 'We need food!'

Four pairs of round black glassy eyes were all fixed upon James.

The Centipede made a wriggling movement with his body as though he were about to glide off the sofa – but he didn't.

There was a long pause – and a long silence.

The Spider (who happened to be a female spider) opened her mouth and ran a long black tongue delicately over her lips. 'Aren't you hungry?' she asked suddenly, leaning forward and addressing herself to James.

Poor James was backed up against the far wall, shivering with fright and much too terrified to answer.

'What's the matter with you?' the Old-Green-Grasshopper asked. 'You look positively ill!'

'He looks as though he's going to faint any second,' the Centipede said.

'Oh, my goodness, the poor thing!' the Ladybird cried. 'I do believe he thinks it's *him* that we are wanting to eat!' There was a roar of laughter from all sides.

'Oh dear, oh dear!' they said. 'What an awful thought!'

'You mustn't be frightened,' the Ladybird said kindly. 'We wouldn't dream of hurting you. You are one of us now, didn't you know that? You are one of the crew. We're all in the same boat.'

'We've been waiting for you all day long,' the Old-Green-Grasshopper said. 'We thought you were never going to turn up. I'm glad you made it.'

'So cheer up, my boy, cheer up!' the Centipede said. 'And meanwhile I wish you'd come over here and give me a hand with these boots. It takes me *hours* to get them all off by myself.'

About Floella

Floella Benjamin was born in the Caribbean on an island called Trinidad on 23rd September 1949. Her father decided to emigrate to England and she came to join him in 1960, when she was 11 years old. Floella's family started their life in Great Britain in Beckenham, South London. Initially she found it very different to her life in Trinidad and growing up in two cultures was challenging.

Floella's mother (Marmie) was a great inspiration to her. She gave her lots of love and encouraged her to do well at school.

Floella always dreamed of becoming a teacher, but instead ended up working in a bank and then later starred in stage musicals. While Floella enjoyed being on stage, she also wanted to try working in television so she auditioned for a variety of roles. Her TV debut was in 1974 in a drama called *Within these Walls* and her success in the show landed her many more roles in TV dramas.

Floella then took on a new role as a presenter of *Play School*, a 1970s children's show. She loved this job and presented the programme for 12 years.

As well as acting and presenting, Floella also loves to sing. She began singing with her dad who had a jazz band.

She often sang with her dad's band and also with large classical orchestras.

In 1987 Floella started her own television production company.

Next page ▶▶▶

Floella has also starred in several pantomimes, worked on numerous radio programmes, narrated audio books and has done voiceovers for a range of adverts and commercials.

Since 1983, Floella has written over 25 children's books.

One book Floella is particularly proud of is one that has been made into a film. *Coming to England* was written in 1995 and is based on her own life. In the book Floella talks about what it's like to be different, to move countries and change cultures and her feelings of rejection. The drama *Coming to England* won a Royal Television Society Award in 2004.

Floella is a keen runner who has completed ten London Marathons for the children's charity Barnardo's. This achievement is even more special as until she turned 50 years old, Floella had never even run at all!

Trekking the Great Wall of China in 2004 in aid of NCH Action for Children is another one of Floella's achievements. She started this in the Gobi Desert and finished 400 km later where the Great Wall meets the Yellow Sea.

Today Floella's passion is for inspiring and helping children and young people. She is a patron and supporter of many charities, including Action for Children and the Sickle Cell Society. In 2008, Floella was inducted into the National Society for the Prevention of Cruelty to Children (NSPCC) Hall of Fame.

Floella supports and empathises with children and young people across the world. Through her charity work, her writing and personal attitudes, she strives to help young people find their identity and to understand where they come from. She hopes all children have a sense of belonging and learn to become proud of themselves.

Macavity

Macavity's a Mystery Cat: he's called the Hidden Paw –
    For he's the master criminal who can defy the Law.
He's the bafflement of Scotland Yard, the Flying Squad's despair:
    For when they reach the scene of crime – *Macavity's not there!*

Macavity, Macavity, there's no one like Macavity,
    He's broken every human law, he breaks the law of gravity.
His powers of levitation would make a fakir stare,
    And when you reach the scene of crime – Macavity's not there!
You may seek him in the basement, you may look up in the air –
    But I tell you once and once again, *Macavity's not there!*

Macavity's a ginger cat, he's very tall and thin;
    You would know him if you saw him, for his eyes are sunken in.
His brow is deeply lined with thought, his head is highly domed;
    His coat is dusty from neglect, his whiskers are uncombed.
He sways his head from side to side, with movements like a snake;
    And when you think he's half asleep, he's always wide awake.

Macavity, Macavity, there's no one like Macavity,
    For he's a fiend in feline shape, a monster of depravity.
You may meet him in a by-street, you may see him in the square –
    But when a crime's discovered, then *Macavity's not there!*

He's outwardly respectable. (They say he cheats at cards.)
    And his footprints are not found in any file of Scotland Yard's.
And when the larder's looted, or the jewel-case is rifled,
    Or when the milk is missing, or another Peke's been stifled,
Or the greenhouse glass is broken, and the trellis past repair –
    Ay, there's the wonder of the thing! *Macavity's not there!*

And when the Foreign Office find a Treaty's gone astray,
    Or the Admiralty lose some plans and drawings by the way,
There may be a scrap of paper in the hall or on the stair –
    But it's useless to investigate – *Macavity's not there!*
And when the loss has been disclosed, the Secret Service say:
    'It *must* have been Macavity!' – but he's a mile away.
You'll be sure to find him resting, or a-licking of his thumbs,
    Or engaged in doing complicated long division sums.

Macavity, Macavity, there's no one like Macavity,
    There never was a Cat of such deceitfulness and suavity.
He always has an alibi, and one or two to spare:
    At whatever time the deed took place – MACAVITY WASN'T THERE!
And they say that all the Cats whose wicked deeds are widely known,
    (I might mention Mungojerrie, I might mention Griddlebone)
Are nothing more than agents for the Cat who all the time
    Just controls their operations: the Napoleon of Crime!

Answers

Set A English reading

A Mad Tea Party

1. Accept either in the garden or in Wonderland. **(1 mark)**
2. She has just drunk a magic potion that makes her small. **(1 mark)**
3. …there's plenty of room. **(1 mark)**
4. the Hare **(1 mark)**
5. polite **(1 mark)**
6. ' …all squashed at one end of a very large table.' **(1 mark)**
7. Any one of the following points:
   - Alice thinks personal remarks are rude.
   - The Hatter's remarks are said very abruptly and to the point.
   - The Hatter's remarks are unprovoked.
   (1 mark)
8. The Mad Hatter begins talking in riddles. **(1 mark)**
9. Any one from: lowers; they become quiet; ends. **(1 mark)**
10. Any one from: confident; friendly; determined; argumentative; sensible. **(1 mark)**
11. Any one from: a narrator; new line for each speaker; stage directions; use of direct language; set as a scene; no speech marks. **(1 mark)**
12. Any one from: it is a tea party which is very unusual; the characters are acting in strange ways; they are saying mad things; they are sitting squashed up; they are talking in riddles; they are offering wine which isn't there. **(1 mark)**
13. Any one from: Alice sits down; looking around the table; in an angry voice; looking up and down at Alice; talking in a sleepy way. **(1 mark)**
14. puzzle **(1 mark)**
15. Any one from: the Narrator sets the scene; moves the story forward; explains what's happening; introduces characters. **(1 mark)**
16. *An Unusual Tea Party* **(1 mark)**

The Isles of Scilly

17. St Mary's **(1 mark)**
18. people live there **(1 mark)**
19. a small aeroplane (Skybus); a passenger ferry (*The Scillonian*)
    (1 mark: both correct for 1 mark)
20. A day visitor with no luggage would be best taking the aeroplane (Skybus) because it's quicker and they would have longer to spend in the Isles of Scilly. They have no luggage so can travel by aeroplane. They will get a good view of all the islands even though they will not get time to see them all on foot. They will be able to choose one of three airports to travel from on the mainland.
    (1 mark for any point from above)
    A family staying for a week who want to see dolphins swimming would be best taking the passenger ferry because they may be able to see dolphins (and basking sharks and sea birds) from the ferry. They are staying a whole week so have plenty of time to spend travelling to Scilly by boat. The family might want to buy food or drinks on board and, as the boat is cheaper, it will cost them less.
    (1 mark for any point from above)
21. There are lots of them, they are not unusual or rare. **(1 mark)**
22. Any of the following answers are acceptable but they must be consistently either 'yes' or 'no'.
    Yes:
    - They are small.
    - Not many cars – good to get away from lots of traffic.
    - Enjoy boats, walking or cycling.
    - Lots of wildlife – birds, fish and plants to see.
    - Lots of tourism.
    - Relaxing; peaceful; quiet.
    - Lovely beaches, sand dunes, rocky coastlines.
    - Varied accommodation.
    - Water sports available.
    - Want to watch the gig races.
    - Would like to explore castles, churches, lighthouses.
    - Would like to visit art galleries, exhibitions, museums, attend concerts.
    - Beautiful islands.
    - Amazing views.
    - Warm climate.
    No:
    - Difficult to get to – you can't drive.

- Very quiet – not many people live there.
- The main town does not have many large facilities.
- Not keen on water, boats or water sports.
- Would prefer somewhere not as warm.
- No interest in birds or wildlife.
- Not much to do.

(1 mark: all three correct for 1 mark)

23. Participating: a participant would sit inside the gig; row; take part in races.

Watching: a spectator would watch the race from a boat, or from the quay on St Mary's; cheer on the gigs.

(2 marks: 1 mark for one participating point, 1 mark for one watching point)

24. Any two of the following:
- maps
- charts
- headings / subheadings
- present tense
- facts are used
- clear language. **(2 marks)**

25. Any three from: walking; bird watching; relaxing on beaches; water sports; visiting historic sites; enjoying the wildlife / plants.

(1 mark for three correct answers)

26. Any two from: walk; ride bicycles; by boat.

(1 mark)

27. a travel leaflet **(1 mark)**

28.

Language used	Explanation of the effect of the language
. . . *flock to the island to race.*	It makes the reader think rowers group like a flock of sheep or birds, and that there are lots of them.
. . . *waiting to be explored* . . .	This phrase gives readers an image of the buildings waiting for people to visit them – really the buildings are just standing there – the author adds interest.
. . . *swirling golden beaches* . . .	Conjures up a picture of the wind gently blowing the sand, which swirls into dunes. 'Golden' makes the reader think of a sunny, warm day, making the beach inviting.

(3 marks)

Street Child

29. A workhouse **(1 mark)**

30. He doesn't know life anywhere else. **(1 mark)**

31. Any one from: so that the children can't escape; so that the children can't see out; so no one can see in. **(1 mark)**

32. Any one from: He could tell the time of year by the weather; the colour of the sky; the light, and dark mornings and nights; he is aware of the change in the seasons. **(1 mark)**

33. He can't stay here forever or for another year; he needs to escape so he will try to run away.

(1 mark for either point)

34. pulled **(1 mark)**

35. Any one from: he knew he had plans to run away; he wasn't going to be there much longer, he had more important things to think about; this would be his last beating so he felt positive and thought he could deal with anything. **(1 mark)**

36. He was afraid they'll get caught and get thrashed. **(1 mark)**

37. **Yes:** Jim is daft for thinking he can escape the workhouse; for running away; for thinking he can go with the big boys – he'll get caught and then get another terrible beating; he has no real plans – where will he sleep? How will he eat?
No: Jim isn't daft for having dreams or for trying to find a way out of the workhouse. **(1 mark)**

38. Look out for each other: 'Don't go, Jim.' Care for each other: 'Tip passed his own share along to him.' Trust each other: Jim told Tip his plans – 'Tip, I'm going to run away today. Come with me?' Strong friendship: they suffer the workhouse together.

(2 marks: award 1 mark for each correct point)

39. He doesn't remember / know life anywhere else. **(1 mark)**

40.

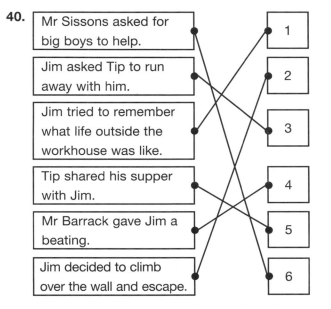

(1 mark for all correct)

41. joy, triumphant

(1 mark: both correct for 1 mark)

42.

Language used	Explanation of the effect of the language
Jim's wild thoughts drummed inside him . . .	The thoughts were pounding away – beating / niggling / constantly there inside him – they were like a drum beat – loud / strong / constant.
. . . the beating inside him was like a wild bird now . . .	His thoughts were getting stronger – like a wild bird's wings – they were spreading out – he was thinking more about it – he couldn't contain his thoughts any more – they needed to escape and fly like a bird – be released.
. . . a shimmer of pain and thrumming wings.	A sudden burst of pain – his 'wings' had been damaged due to the beating he had just endured – he was hurt.

(3 marks: 1 mark for each correct box)

Set A English grammar, punctuation and spelling

Paper 1: questions

1. an elephant; a superhero

    (1 mark: both correct for 1 mark)

2. discover **(1 mark)**

3. We **was** /(were) going to play outside on our bikes. I **done** /(did) well in my maths test this morning. **(1 mark)**

4. "Wait for me!" shouted Orla.
    "Ouch! My hand hurts."
    Freddie whispered, "Are you scared?" **(1 mark)**

5. Olivia and Sandip (were building) sandcastles at the beach. **(1 mark)**

6. The authors wrote letters to the newspaper.

    (1 mark)

7. Nottingham is located in the East Midlands. The river that runs through Nottingham is called the River Trent. **(1 mark)**

8. (Since) it was very cold outside, Sam decided to fasten his coat. **(1 mark)**

9.

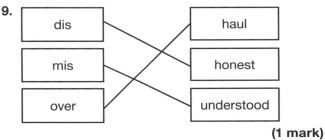

(1 mark)

10. Emma's cat had five kittens last night.
    The boys' changing rooms were locked.
    Jamie's lunchbox was left overnight in his classroom. **(1 mark)**

11. William Shakespeare – a famous author – wrote the play 'Macbeth'. **(1 mark)**

12. Although she is younger than me, my sister is much taller. **(1 mark)**

13. Any suitable adverbials of time, e.g. First; Then; Next, followed by a comma. **(1 mark)**

14. You've been learning about materials in science, haven't you? **(1 mark)**

15. While the band was playing, I was dancing with my friends. **(1 mark)**

16. therefore **(1 mark)**

17. Feeling confident, the pianist played to a room full of people. **(1 mark)**

18. whipped **(1 mark)**

19. pronoun **(1 mark)**

20. I will wash the car today. **(1 mark)**

21.

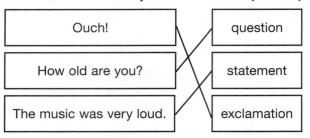

Ouch!		question
How old are you?		statement
The music was very loud.		exclamation

(1 mark: all correct for 1 mark)

22. (he) **(1 mark)**

23. Later that evening, we said goodbye and began our journey home. **(1 mark)**

24. Mangoes, kiwis, apples, pineapples and strawberries are all types of fruit.
(1 mark: all correct for 1 mark)

25. We laughed at each other's funny jokes. **(1 mark)**

26. I am allowed to watch television (while) eating my dinner. **(1 mark)**

27. Answers may vary. Examples:

	Synonym	Antonym
sad	unhappy	happy
rich	wealthy	poor
big	large	small
old	ancient	new

(1 mark)

28. The skateboard park, located behind the playground, is to be used by children who are over eight. **Or** The skateboard park (located behind the playground) is to be used by children who are over eight. **Or** The skateboard park – located behind the playground – is to be used by children who are over eight. **(1 mark)**

29. On your marks . . . ready . . . steady . . . go! **(1 mark)**

30. The historians visited the ancient ruins. **(1 mark)**

31.

Noun	Verb
simplification	to simplify
calculation	to calculate
magnification	to magnify

(1 mark)

32. The girl walked (up) the stairs. **(1 mark)**

33. Any correct addition of a subordinate clause will be award a mark, e.g. Despite the cold, rainy morning, the farmer went into his field; The farmer, who owned several acres of land, went into his field. **(1 mark)**

34. My uncle, who lives in France, came to visit us at Christmas. **Or** My uncle who lives in France came to visit us at Christmas. **Or** At Christmas, my uncle who lives in France came to visit us. **Or** At Christmas, my uncle, who lives in France, came to visit us. **(1 mark)**

35. The old lady who was shouting at her neighbour was feeling angry. **(1 mark)**

36. Any suitable question starting with a capital letter and ending with a question mark, e.g. How does Joel get to school? **(1 mark)**

37. (Put) (Mix) **(1 mark: both correct for 1 mark)**

38. He **(1 mark)**

39. Any one from: can't; won't; didn't; don't; couldn't; wouldn't. **(1 mark)**

40.

| to dance | | to smile |

When I was dancing in the show I was smiling all the time.

(2 marks: 1 mark for each correct word)

41. "What time does the train leave the station?" Mary asked the guard.
"Three minutes past ten" the guard answered.
(1 mark for both sentences correct)

42. 'Where are you going' the bus driver asked.

| ✓ |

(1 mark)

43. The books **and** DVDs need returning to the library on Monday **or** Tuesday **but** remember it is closed each day for lunch. **(1 mark for all correct)**

44. While I was waiting to see the doctor, I read a book. **(1 mark)**

45. The cat – fast asleep on the rug – was keeping warm by the fire. **(1 mark)**

46. With his sports kit on, Tom was ready for the game. **(1 mark)**

47. If the bus were late again, the children would be cross. **(1 mark)**

48.

Noun	Adjective
child	childish/childlike
courage	courageous
despair	desperate
hope	hopeful
caution	cautious

(1 mark)

49. around **(1 mark)**

50. went; were **(1 mark)**

Paper 2: Spelling

These are the correct spellings:

1. shoulder
2. weather
3. naughty
4. fruit
5. treasure
6. return
7. country
8. supermarket
9. equipment
10. temperature
11. infectious
12. competition
13. average
14. cereal
15. confident
16. artificial
17. changeable
18. draught
19. immediately
20. committee

Set B English reading

James and the Giant Peach

1. a simile **(1 mark)**
2. Any one of the following: terrified; scared; worried; unsure; frightened. **(1 mark)**
3. closely **(1 mark)**
4.

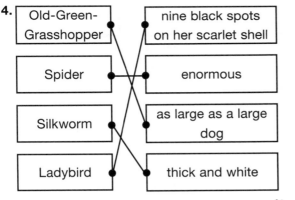

(1 mark)

5. Any one from: charge back; race back; go very quickly. **(1 mark)**
6. The Ladybird thinks James is thinking that the creatures want to eat him. **(1 mark)**
7. You have joined us now, you are just the same as us and we will treat you as our friend / family. You are no different from us – we are all here together. **(1 mark)**

8.

	True	False
A fence surrounded the peach.	✓	
The tunnel was dry and cold.		✓
James bumped his head on the stone in the middle of the peach.	✓	
James couldn't stand up because the peach wasn't big enough.		✓
The creatures were at least the same size as James.	✓	

(1 mark: all five correct for 1 mark)

9. Author is creating suspense. What is going to happen next? Telling us there were four creatures staring, the word 'fixed' creates the image – they were all looking at James, nothing else. The author is helping readers understand the anxiety James must be feeling.

(2 marks: 1 mark for each point made)

10. Use of personification – 'the garden lay', 'the whole garden seemed to be alive with magic'. Use of the word 'moonlight' – creating atmosphere, implying that something exciting, unusual, magical is about to happen. Use of similes – visual imagery such as 'sparkling and twinkling like diamonds'.

(2 marks: 1 mark for each point made)

11. The Centipede has many feet so has a lot of boots to take off. **(1 mark)**
12. head and shoulders

(1 mark: both correct for 1 mark)

13. Answers will vary. Examples: damp; wet. **(1 mark)**
14. excited **(1 mark)**
15. Old-Green-Grasshopper and Ladybird

(1 mark: both correct for 1 mark)

About Floella

16. biography **(1 mark)**
17. Accept either in the Caribbean or Trinidad.

1 mark)

18. Any one from: very difficult; hard work; a struggle.

(1 mark)

19. Mum: Floella's mother (Marmie) was a great inspiration to her; gave her lots of love; encouraged her.
Dad: She began singing with her dad; she often sang with her dad's jazz band.

(2 marks: 1 mark for point made for mum, 1 mark for point made for dad)

20. *Coming to England* **(1 mark)**
21. *Within these Walls* **(1 mark)**

22.

Event	Date
Born	1949
Came to England	1960
Made her TV debut	1974
Started her own television production company	1987
Wrote *Coming to England*	1995
Trekked the Great Wall of China	2004

(2 marks: 1 mark if four or five answers are correct, 2 marks if all six answers are correct)

23. chronological **(1 mark)**

24. Barnardo's **(1 mark)**

25. Any two from: factual; pictures; true statements.
(1 mark)

26. Completed ten London Marathons for Barnardo's; trekked the Great Wall of China for NCH Action for Children worked and raised money for the NSPCC.
(2 marks for three correct answers; 1 mark for two correct)

27.

	Fact	Opinion
She worked in a bank.	✓	
She loved her job on *Play School*.		✓
She presented *Play School* for 12 years.	✓	
She has completed ten London Marathons.	✓	
She is a keen runner.		✓

(1 mark: all correct for 1 mark)

28. Because Floella moved to a new culture when she was a child she is aware of the difficulties children face in this situation; she wants to help children in a similar position; to help them find their identity; and for them to understand where they came from.
(2 marks: 1 mark for any two points made)

Macavity

29. Macavity's not there. **(1 mark)**

30. appearance **(1 mark)**

31. Any one from: uncared for; left alone; not looked after. **(1 mark)**

32. Whenever a crime has been committed Macavity is always involved but he hides away to keep out of trouble so his whereabouts are a mystery to those looking for him. **(1 mark)**

33. Macavity's absence is one of the main points of the poem. Repetition of this phrase emphasises this point. **(1 mark)**

34. He always has an explanation for where he was at the time of the crime – sometimes he has more than one explanation. **(1 mark)**

35. narrative **(1 mark)**

36. The poet uses rhyme for effect – it is regular throughout each verse. Rhyming couplets are used. The poem has even rhyme, which helps the poem to be read / performed easily.
(1 mark for any point from the above)

37. By the end of the poem, the poet is fed up of telling us that Macavity is not there . . . we know by now that he wasn't there. The capital letters indicate volume, as if he's driving the point home. **(1 mark)**

38.

	Fact	Opinion
It is fun watching Macavity cause trouble.		✓
Macavity's a ginger cat.	✓	
His coat is dusty.	✓	
Macavity has no-one to care for him.		✓

(1 mark: all correct for 1 mark)

39. 'movements like a snake' **(1 mark)**

40. looted **(1 mark)**

41. Any one from: Macavity acts as the boss, the ringleader; he controls the crimes the other cats do; he's the best; the one in charge.
(1 mark)

42. Any three suitable answers from:
- Macavity runs away from trouble.
- Macavity is a naughty cat – he breaks all the rules.
- He is a street cat – he always looks neglected.
- He is outwardly respectable – he tricks people.
- He controls the other cats – he's in charge.
- Macavity is sly.
- It is always Macavity who has committed or organised the crime. **(3 marks)**

Set B English grammar, punctuation and spelling

Paper 1: questions

1. The (creepy) shadows darted quickly past the (wooden) fence, along the (hidden) path and into the (gloomy) garage. **(1 mark for all correct)**

2. because **(1 mark)**

3. (did) ; (have) **(1 mark for both correct)**

4. The dog's tail was wagging.

   The boys' coats were on the floor.

   The women's changing rooms were busy.
   (1 mark for all correct)

5. After the singing, Kenzie blew out the candles.
   (1 mark)

6. Any correct answer, e.g.

   The busy skateboard park.

   The skiing holiday. **(1 mark for all correct)**

7. ellipses **(1 mark)**

8. Grace bought a bouncy ball; she played with it in the garden. **(1 mark)**

9.

Sentence	Proper noun	Common noun
My birthday is in January.	✓	
The bees landed on the flower.		✓
The car towed the caravan.		✓
His brother's name is Andrew.	✓	

(1 mark for all correct)

10. Any suitable modal verb, e.g. should; ought (to) **(1 mark)**

11. noun = 'celebration' **(1 mark)**

12.

Rosie climbed the stairs.	passive
The stairs were climbed by Rosie.	active

(1 mark for both correct)

13. The girls were tired (but) it was too early to go to bed. **(1 mark)**

14. "You were expecting this letter today, (weren't you?)" **(1 mark)**

15. The ice cream van that is in the car park is very popular today. **(1 mark)**

16. She walked along the canal path.

    The dog hid under the table.

    I was lost in the maze. **(1 mark for all correct)**

17. The little boy watched TV and ate a sandwich.
    (1 mark)

18. (An) alligator is (a) large reptile.
    (1 mark for both correct)

19. Rosie's homework was too hard for **her** and **she** felt sad that **she** couldn't do **it**.
    (1 mark for all correct)

20. He will go to school tomorrow. **(1 mark)**

21. Isn't it?; don't you?
    (1 mark for both correct)

22. Mrs Jones (the Year 5 teacher) played the piano in school today. **(1 mark)**

23. Any suitable subordinate clauses, e.g. Although I didn't have much time, I went to the park.
    (1 mark)

24. Hanging upside down, the bat made loud noises as the night sky grew darker. **(1 mark)**

25. Any suitable words, e.g.

Word	Synonym	Antonym
stiff	rigid	bendy
angry	cross	calm

(1 mark for all words if correct)

26. The tree **sway** / (**sways**) gently in the breeze.

    The goats (**have**) / **has** two horns each.

    The children (**are**) / **is** too noisy!
    (1 mark for all correct)

27. To make a pop-up book you will need three things:

    • scissors

    • card

    • glue

    (Accept full-stop after each word. Accept capital letter at start of each word)
    (1 mark: 1 mark if all bullet points are correct)

28. Any three from:

    dis / re / un   cover

    re   place

    dis   allow   **(1 mark for all correct)**

29. I like drawing **and** painting **but / although** my sister prefers writing.
    (1 mark for both correct)

30. After tea, we went to the cinema.
    (1 mark for correct adverbial and correct punctuation)

31. "There will be an important visitor in assembly," Mrs Shepherd told her class. **Or** Mrs Shepherd told her class, "There will be an important visitor in assembly." **(1 mark)**

32. The milkman delivers fresh produce on a Monday, Tuesday, Thursday and Saturday. **(1 mark)**

33. Noah and **I** went for a walk in the woods. Our parents told my sister and **me** to hurry up. **(1 mark)**

34. The cat slept (in) the warm, cosy basket. **(1 mark)**

35. Ella played the piano; Alex played the flute. **(1 mark)**

36.

Adverbial	Time (when)	Place (where)
frequently	✓	
regularly	✓	
often	✓	
in the middle of		✓

(1 mark for all correct)

37. Brighton, which is a seaside town, is located on the south coast of England. **(1 mark)**

38. My best friend, Hayley, who loves dogs, was thrilled when she got a puppy for her birthday. **Or** My best friend Hayley, who loves dogs, was thrilled when she got a puppy for her birthday. **(1 mark)**

39. 'It's my turn next,' I told my older brother. **(1 mark)**

40. should've; they'll; he's **(1 mark for all correct)**

41. During his stay on the farm, Jon saw some ducks, a herd of goats and a huge, pink pig. Accept a colon after 'saw'. **(1 mark)**

42.

Explanation	True	False
A request is to ask for something.	✓	
An indulgent is an invitation.		✓
A container is used to put things in.	✓	
A bleak morning is a dismal one.	✓	

(1 mark for all correct)

43. to laugh; to walk; to fly; to grow **(1 mark for all correct)**

44. I have not got any / I've not got any. **(1 mark)**

45.

Verb	Noun
agree	agreement
refer	referral / reference / referee
form	formation / formality
assist	assistant / assistance

(1 mark for all correct)

46. end **(1 mark)**

47. We should have stayed late at school tonight. **(1 mark)**

48. I was eating all my dinner. **(1 mark)**

49. Annie's mum worked at the school library. The apostrophe is used for possession to show that the mum belongs to Annie. **(1 mark for correct use of apostrophe and for correct explanation)**

50. were **(1 mark)**

Paper 2: Spelling

These are the correct spellings:

1. island
2. delicious
3. potatoes
4. promise
5. favourite
6. weight
7. various
8. adorable
9. opportunity
10. relevant
11. persuade
12. stomach
13. curiosity
14. awkward
15. vehicle
16. mourning
17. stationary
18. caffeine
19. transferred
20. accommodation

Spelling Test Administration

The instructions below are for the spelling tests.

Read the following instruction out to your child:

I am going to read 20 sentences to you. Each sentence has a word missing. Listen carefully to the missing word and fill this in the answer space, making sure that you spell it correctly.

I will read the word, then the word within a sentence, then repeat the word a third time.

You should now read the spellings three times, as given below. Leave at least a 12-second gap between spellings. At the end, read all the sentences again, giving your child the chance to make any changes they wish to their answers.

Set A English grammar, punctuation and spelling

Paper 2: spelling

Spelling 1: The word is **shoulder**. Jai hurt his **shoulder** playing tennis with his friends.
The word is **shoulder**.

Spelling 2: The word is **weather**. The **weather** forecast for today is mostly sunny and warm.
The word is **weather**.

Spelling 3: The word is **naughty**. Our **naughty** little kitten had scratched the carpet.
The word is **naughty**.

Spelling 4: The word is **fruit**. Mangoes, pineapples, kiwis and oranges are all types of **fruit**.
The word is **fruit**.

Spelling 5: The word is **treasure**. We are going on a **treasure** hunt tomorrow.
The word is **treasure**.

Spelling 6: The word is **return**. The new clothes didn't fit so I need to **return** them to the shop.
The word is **return**.

Spelling 7: The word is **country**. My ambition is to play football for my **country**.
The word is **country.**

Spelling 8: The word is **supermarket**.
The **supermarket** was extremely busy this afternoon.
The word is **supermarket**.

Spelling 9: The word is **equipment**. At break time, we play with the outdoor **equipment**.
The word is **equipment**.

Spelling 10: The word is **temperature**.
The **temperature** water boils at is 100 degrees Celsius.
The word is **temperature**.

Spelling 11: The word is **infectious**. The doctor said the rash was highly **infectious**.
The word is **infectious**.

Spelling 12: The word is **competition**.
Sam won a **competition** he entered at school.
The word is **competition**.

Spelling 13: The word is **average**. Jemima was an **average** height for her age.
The word is **average**.

Spelling 14: The word is **cereal**. Our family eats **cereal** for breakfast.
The word is **cereal**.

Spelling 15: The word is **confident**. The actress was very **confident** on the stage.
The word is **confident**.

Spelling 16: The word is **artificial**. The flowers in the bathroom are **artificial**.
The word is **artificial**.

Spelling 17: The word is **changeable**. The weather is very **changeable** today.
The word is **changeable**.

Spelling 18: The word is **draught**. There is a **draught** coming from the large window.
The word is **draught**.

Spelling 19: The word is **immediately**.
The building must be evacuated **immediately** if the fire alarm rings.
The word is **immediately**.

Spelling 20: The word is **committee**. The **committee** members all attended a meeting at the school last night.
The word is **committee**.

Set B English grammar, punctuation and spelling

Paper 2: spelling

Spelling 1: The word is **island**. The **island** of Majorca is close to Spain.
The word is **island**.

Spelling 2: The word is **delicious**. The chocolate cake was **delicious**. The word is **delicious**.

Spelling 3: The word is **potatoes**. **Potatoes** can be mashed, chipped, boiled or baked.
The word is **potatoes**.

Spelling 4: The word is **promise**. A **promise** should never be broken! The word is **promise**.

Spelling 5: The word is **favourite**. My **favourite** sport is cricket. The word is **favourite**.

Spelling 6: The word is **weight**. The **weight** of the luggage is less than 15 kilograms. The word is **weight**.

Spelling 7: The word is **various**. **Various** teachers have told me I have a talent for drawing. The word is **various**.

Spelling 8: The word is **adorable**. The kittens are **adorable**. The word is **adorable**.

Spelling 9: The word is **opportunity**. Playing football for the school team is a great **opportunity**. The word is **opportunity**.

Spelling 10: The word is **relevant**. All the **relevant** information should be underlined. The word is **relevant**.

Spelling 11: The word is **persuade**. I am trying to **persuade** my mum to buy me some new boots. The word is **persuade**.

Spelling 12: The word is **stomach**. My **stomach** feels full after lunch. The word is **stomach**.

Spelling 13: The word is **curiosity**. Mata listened to the story with **curiosity**. The word is **curiosity**.

Spelling 14: The word is **awkward**. The first time we met was a little **awkward**. The word is **awkward**.

Spelling 15: The word is **vehicle**. Ned's **vehicle** was the fastest. The word is **vehicle**.

Spelling 16: The word is **mourning**. The whole family is in **mourning** for our pet. The word is **mourning**.

Spelling 17: The word is **stationary**. Because of the roadworks, the traffic was **stationary**. The word is **stationary**.

Spelling 18: The word is **caffeine**. Coffee and fizzy drinks usually contain **caffeine**. The word is **caffeine**.

Spelling 19: The word is **transferred**. The gymnasts **transferred** their weight across the bars. The word is **transferred**.

Spelling 20: The word is **accommodation**. We do not mind what type of **accommodation** we stay in on holiday. The word is **accommodation**.

KS2 Success

Age 7-11

Maths

Test
Practice Papers

Trevor Dixon

Contents

(pull-out section at the back of the book)

Introduction and instructions

How these tests will help your child

This book is made up of two complete sets of practice test papers. Each set contains similar test papers to those that your child will take at the end of Year 6 in maths. They can be used any time throughout the year to provide practice for the Key Stage 2 tests.

The results of both sets of papers will provide a good idea of the strengths and weaknesses of your child.

Administering the tests

- Provide your child with a quiet environment where they can complete each test undisturbed.
- Provide your child with a pen or pencil, ruler, eraser and protractor. A calculator is **not** allowed.
- The amount of time given for each test varies, so remind your child at the start of each one how long they have and give them access to a clock or watch.
- You should only read the instructions out to your child, not the actual questions.
- Although handwriting is not assessed, remind your child that their answers should be clear.
- Advise your child that if they are unable to do one of the questions they should go on to the next one and come back to it later, if they have time. If they finish before the end, they should go back and check their work.

Paper 1: arithmetic

- Answers are worth 1 or 2 marks, with a total number of 40 marks. Long multiplication and long division questions are worth 2 marks each. A mark may be awarded for showing the correct method.
- Your child will have **30 minutes** to answer the questions as quickly and carefully as they can.
- Encourage your child to look at the number of marks after each question to help them find out how much detail is required in their answer.
- Where questions are expressed as common fractions, the answers should be given as common fractions. All other answers should be given as whole or decimal numbers.

Paper 2 and Paper 3: reasoning

- Answers are worth 1 or 2 marks, with a total number of 35 marks. A mark may be awarded for showing the correct method in specific questions where there is a method box.
- Your child will have **40 minutes** to answer the questions as quickly and carefully as they can.
- Encourage your child to look at the number of marks after each question to help them find out how much detail is required in their answer.
- If your child needs to do some working out, advise them that they can use the space around the question.

Marking the practice test papers

The answers and mark scheme have been provided to enable you to check how your child has performed. Fill in the marks that your child achieved for each part of the tests.

Please note: these tests are **only a guide** to the level or mark your child can achieve and cannot guarantee the same level is achieved during the Key Stage 2 tests.

	Set A	**Set B**
Paper 1: arithmetic	/ 40	/ 40
Paper 2: reasoning	/ 35	/ 35
Paper 3: reasoning	/ 35	/ 35
Total	/ 110	/ 110

These scores roughly correspond with these levels: up to 49 = well below required level; 50–69 = below required level; 70–89 = meets required level; 90–110 = exceeds required level.

When an area of weakness has been identified, it is useful to go over it and to look at similar types of questions with your child. Sometimes your child will be familiar with the subject matter but might not understand what the question is asking. This will become apparent when talking to your child.

Shared marking and target setting

Engaging your child in the marking process will help them to develop a greater understanding of the tests and, more importantly, provide them with some ownership of their learning. They will be able to see more clearly how and why certain areas have been identified for them to target for improvement.

Top tips for your child

Don't make silly mistakes. Make sure you emphasize to your child the importance of reading the question. Easy marks can be picked up by just doing as the question asks.

Make answers clearly legible. If your child has made a mistake, encourage them to put a cross through it and write the correct answer clearly next to it. Try to encourage your child to use an eraser as little as possible.

Don't panic! These practice test papers, and indeed the end of Key Stage 2 tests, are meant to provide a guide to the level a child has attained. They are not the be-all and end-all, as children are assessed regularly throughout the school year. Explain to your child that there is no need to worry if they cannot do a question – tell them to go on to the next question and come back to the problematic question later if they have time.

Key Stage 2

Maths

Paper 1: arithmetic

You **may not** use a calculator to answer any questions in this test paper.

Time:

You have **30 minutes** to complete this test paper.

Maximum mark	Actual mark
40	

First name	
Last name	

Date of birth	Day		Month		Year	

1

$43 \times 5 =$

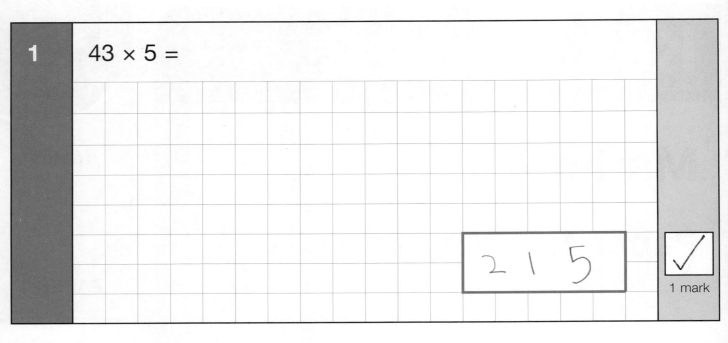

2 1 5

2

$574 + 56 =$

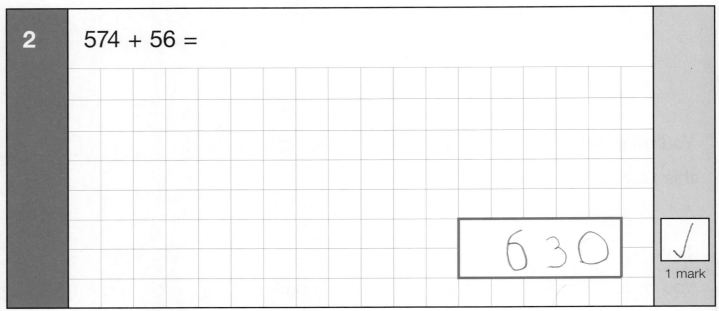

6 3 0

3

$1,234 + 100 =$

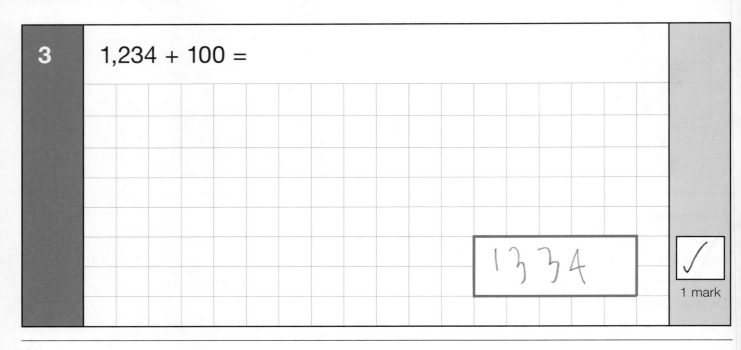

1 3 3 4

4	$\dfrac{2}{5} + \dfrac{2}{5} =$		
		$\dfrac{4}{5}$	✓ 1 mark

5	9,999 – 1,000 =		
		8 9 9 9	✓ 1 mark

6	5,868 – 2,434 =		
		3 4 3 4	✓ 1 mark

7	607 × 3 =

1 8 2 1

1 mark

8	8.1 ÷ 10 =

0.81

1 mark

9	45,054 + 32,876 =

77930

77300

1 mark

10

$5^2 = 5 \times 5$ $5^3 = 5 \times 5 \times 5$

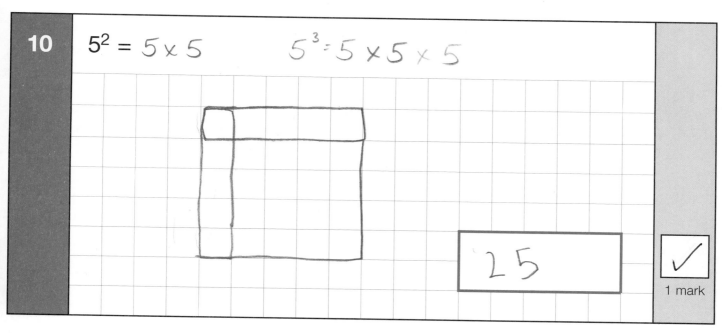

25

1 mark

11

$9,345 \div 3 =$

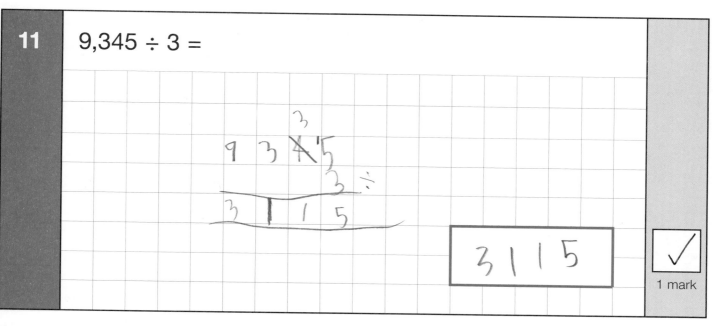

3115

1 mark

12

$\dfrac{9}{10} - \dfrac{1}{5} =$

$\dfrac{7}{10}$

1 mark

13   10 − 15 =

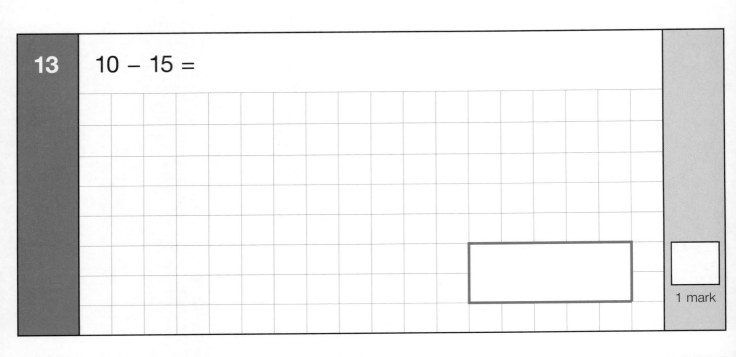

1 mark

14 $\dfrac{1}{2} + \dfrac{2}{5} =$

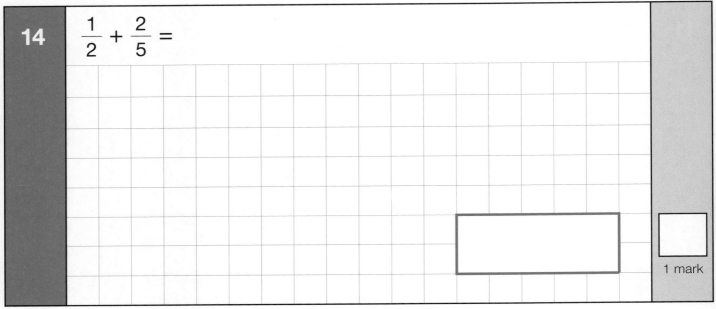

1 mark

15 $\dfrac{1}{3} \times \dfrac{1}{2} =$

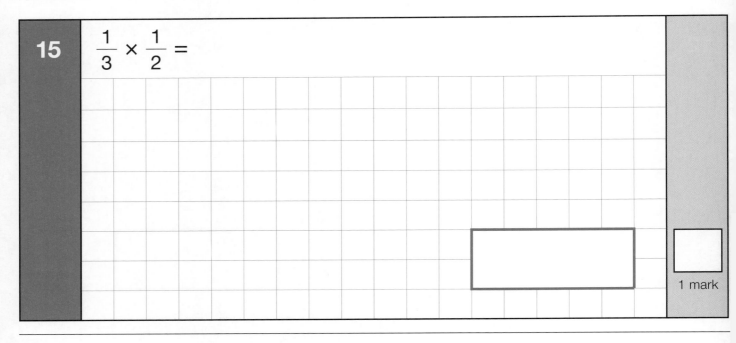

1 mark

16 $\frac{1}{2} \div 4 =$

1 mark

17 $0.6 \times 4 =$

1 mark

18 $50\% \text{ of } 2{,}500 =$

1 mark

19

50 − 5 × 10 =

1 mark

20

45,725 + 63,750 =

1 mark

21

825,804 − 235,075 =

1 mark

22   47.32 + 215.44 =

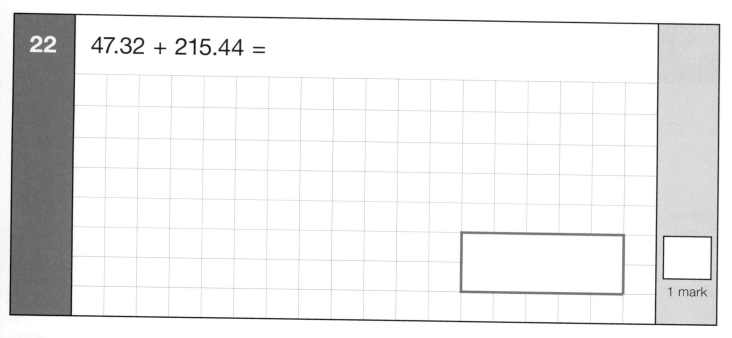

1 mark

23   486.48 − 39.57 =

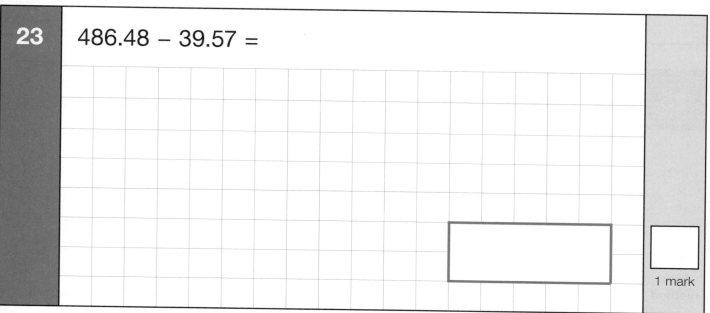

1 mark

24

Show your method

```
    2 3 4
  ×   2 6
  ─────────
```


2 marks

25

Show your method

```
2 3 ) 5 5 2
```


2 marks

26	30.75 × 100 =	
		1 mark

27	$\dfrac{3}{4} + \dfrac{4}{12} =$	
		1 mark

28	78.7 − 65.88 =	
		1 mark

29   ☐ = 65 ÷ 100

30   50.806 − 32.661 =

31

Show your method

$$\begin{array}{r} 5\ 7\ 3 \\ \times \quad 4\ 5 \\ \hline \end{array}$$

2 marks

32

$$\frac{3}{5} \div 4 =$$

1 mark

33

3 5 | 8 7 5

Show
your
method

2 marks

34

$40 \times 1\frac{1}{2} =$

1 mark

35

$$\frac{1}{3} \times \frac{1}{5} =$$

1 mark

36

56.77 − 5.777 =

1 mark

Key Stage 2

Maths

Paper 2: reasoning

You **may not** use a calculator to answer any questions in this test paper.

Time:

You have **40 minutes** to complete this test paper.

Maximum mark	Actual mark
35	....

First name	
Last name	

Date of birth	Day		Month		Year	

1 This is part of a number square.

Circle the numbers that give a remainder of 3 when divided by 8

43	44	45	46	47
53	54	55	56	57
63	64	65	66	67
73	74	75	76	77
83	84	85	86	87

2 marks

2 Draw a pentagon with a pair of parallel lines.

Use a ruler.

2 marks

3 Ellie and Rosie buy two pizzas.

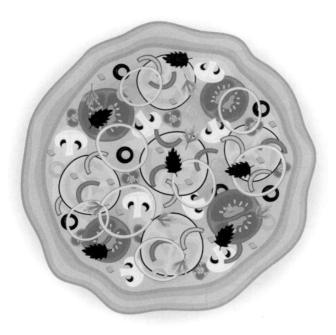 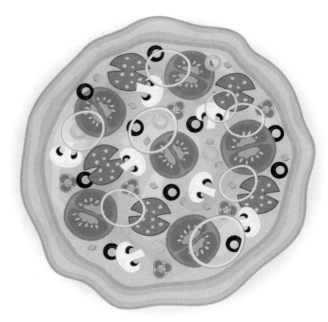

Ellie eats $\frac{5}{8}$ of her pizza.

Rosie eats $\frac{7}{8}$ of her pizza.

What fraction of one pizza is left?

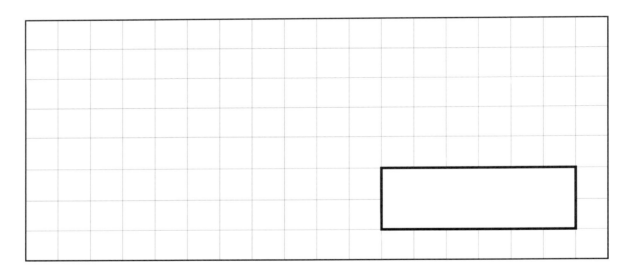

1 mark

Tick (✔) the two numbers that have a difference of 1000

32,658 ☐

33,758 ☐

33,768 ☐

34,758 ☐

43,858 ☐

1 mark

5 Write the missing numbers in this calculation.

```
      5  ☐  4  ☐
   +  ☐  5  ☐  4
   _____
   1  2  6  0  0
```

1 mark

6 Calculate the perimeter of this shape.

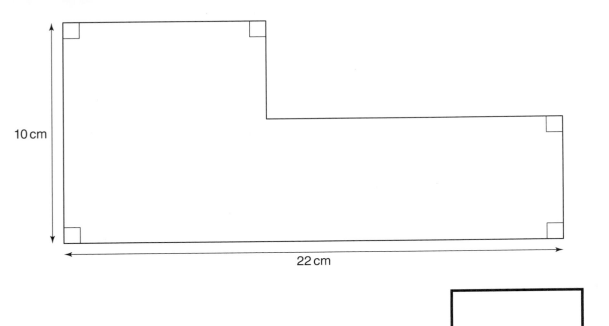

10 cm

22 cm

7 A number squared and a number cubed both equal 64

Find the numbers.

$\boxed{}^2 = 64 = \boxed{}^3$

8 Four hundred and sixty thousand, three hundred and five.

Write this number in digits.

1 mark

9

Reflect the shape in the mirror line.

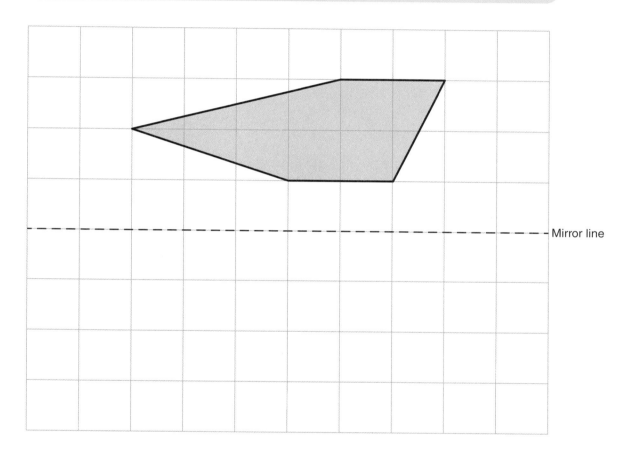

Mirror line

1 mark

10 This table gives approximate conversions between kilograms and pounds.

kilograms	pounds
1	2.2
2	4.4
4	8.8
8	17.6
16	35.2

Use the table to convert 7 kilograms into pounds.

pounds

1 mark

Use the table to convert 22 pounds into kilograms.

kg

1 mark

11 The attendance at a football match was 48,139

Two newspaper reports rounded this attendance in two different ways.

The Globe gave the attendance to the nearest hundred.

What was the attendance given?

1 mark

The Planet gave the attendance to the nearest ten thousand.

What was the attendance given?

1 mark

12 Tick (✔) the largest number.

56.276　　　56.093　　　56.239　　　56.198　　　56.273

☐　　　　☐　　　　☐　　　　☐　　　　☐

1 mark

13 Tom and Jack collect football cards.

Tom has 5 coloured cards to every 3 black and white cards.

If Tom has 36 black and white cards, how many coloured cards does he have?

☐

1 mark

Jack has 6 coloured cards to every 5 black and white cards.

If Jack has 36 coloured cards, how many cards does he have altogether?

☐

1 mark

14 $330 \div 8 =$

Give your answer as a decimal.

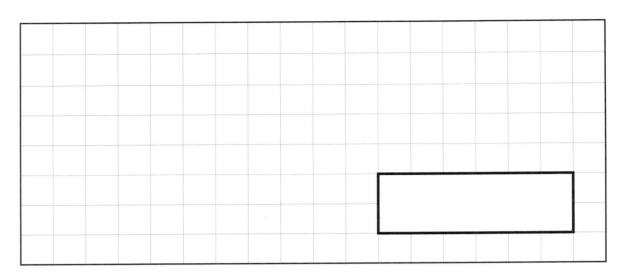

1 mark

15 Oakview School has 460 pupils.

40% are girls.

Sea Lane School has 240 pupils.

60% are girls.

How many more girls are there at Oakview School?

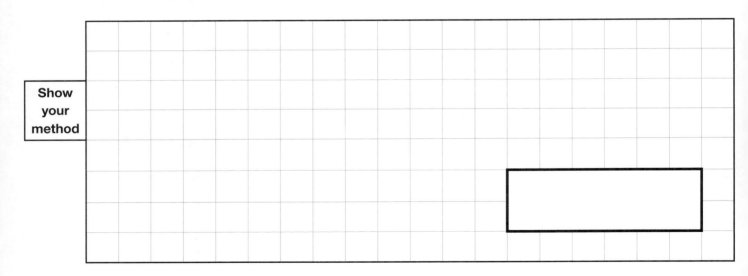

Show your method

3 marks

16 Find the value of $5a - 2b$, when $a = 5$ and $b = 7$

Find the value of $5a + 2b$, when $a = 7$ and $b = 5$

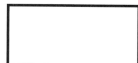

17 Here are two equations with missing numbers.

$$\square + \triangle = 18$$

$$\square - \triangle = 6$$

Work out the value of the missing numbers.

$$\square = \boxed{}$$

$$\triangle = \boxed{}$$

18 Here are four containers holding some water.

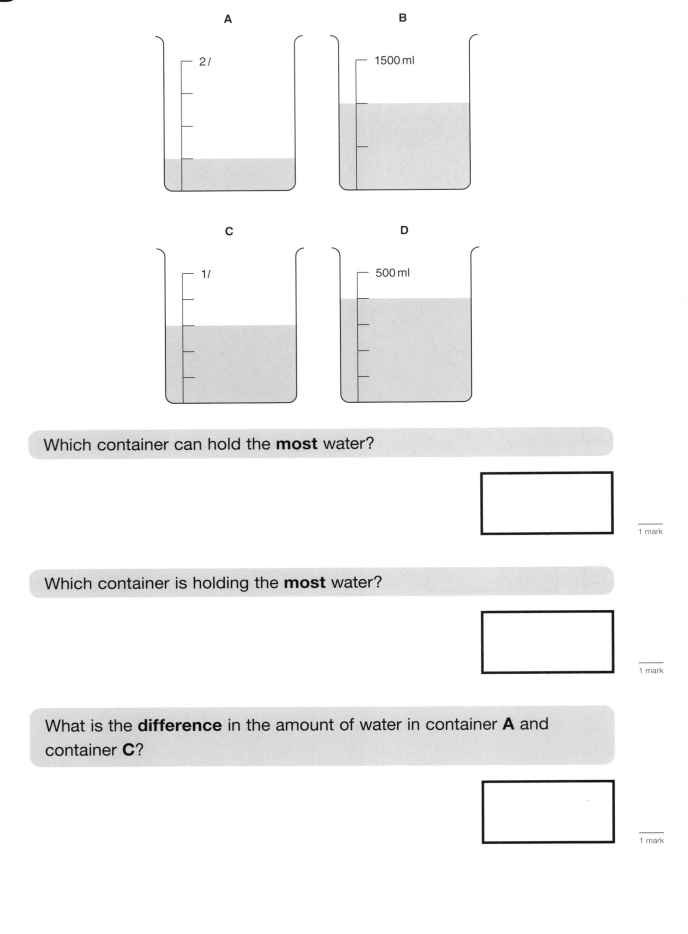

Which container can hold the **most** water?

1 mark

Which container is holding the **most** water?

1 mark

What is the **difference** in the amount of water in container **A** and container **C**?

1 mark

19 Tick (✔) the circle with a radius as a dotted line.

| | | | | 1 mark |

20 Here is a set of numbers.

7   15   24   30   48   53

Which two numbers are **common multiples** of 3 and 4?

[   ] and [   ]

1 mark

Which two numbers are **common factors** of 60?

[   ] and [   ]

1 mark

Which two numbers are **prime numbers**?

[   ] and [   ]

1 mark

21 Sally wanted to go on holiday to Spain.

She compared the mean temperatures for UK and Spain.

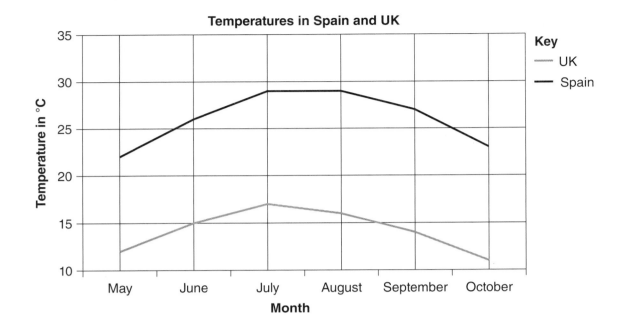

How much **warmer** was it in Spain than in UK in September?

°C

1 mark

Sally wants to go to Spain when it is closest to 25°C.

Which months could Sally choose?

1 mark

Key Stage 2

Maths

Paper 3: reasoning

You **may not** use a calculator to answer any questions in this test paper.

Time:

You have **40 minutes** to complete this test paper.

Maximum mark	Actual mark
35	

First name	
Last name	

Date of birth	Day		Month		Year	

1   What number is shown by this abacus?

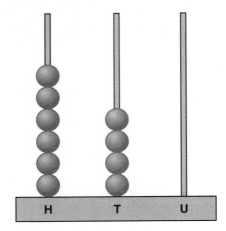

H   T   U

1 mark

2   Find the missing number.

$9 \times \boxed{} = 72 \div 2$

1 mark

3

What time is shown on this clock?

1 mark

4 Part of this shape is missing.

The dotted line is a line of symmetry.

Complete the shape.

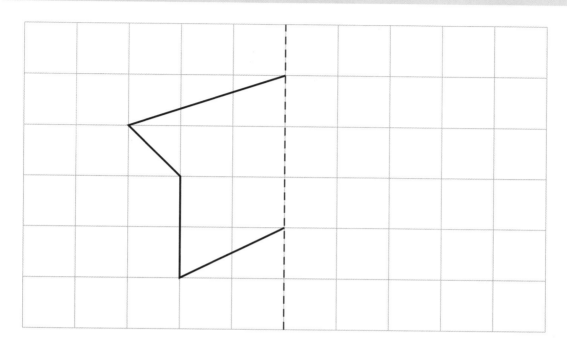

1 mark

Draw the line of symmetry on this shape.

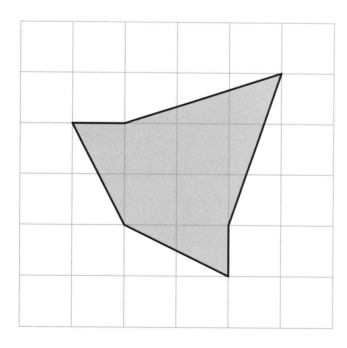

1 mark

5 Chloe has 217 minutes left on her phone.

She uses 83 minutes.

She gets another 350 minutes.

How many minutes does Chloe have on her phone?

Show your method													
												minutes	

2 marks

6 Tom buys 5 identical books for £26.

What is the cost of each book?

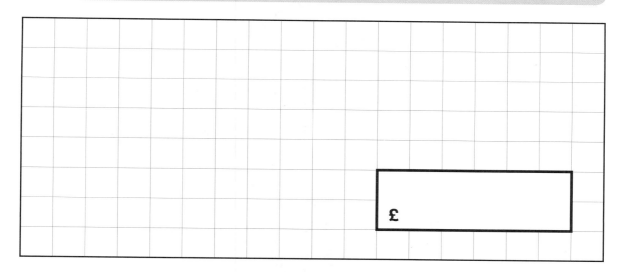

£

1 mark

7 1 inch is about 2.5 centimetres.

How many centimetres is 12 inches?

cm

1 mark

There are 12 inches in 1 foot.

There are 3 feet in 1 yard.

Is a yard shorter or longer than 1 metre?

Explain how you know.

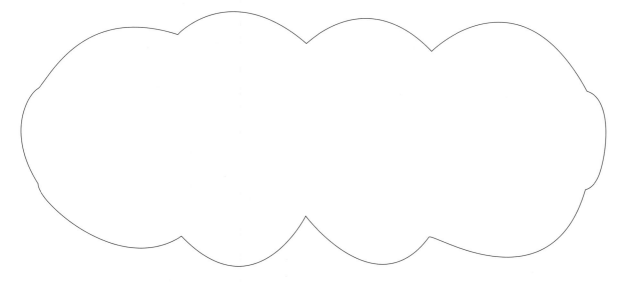

1 mark

8 The temperature outside a greenhouse is −4°C.

The temperature inside the greenhouse is 4°C.

What is the difference between the two temperatures?

°C

9 Two prime numbers total 31.

What are the two numbers?

List the prime numbers that are greater than 40 and less than 50.

10 Manisha has 24 counters.

- $\frac{1}{4}$ of the counters are red.

- $\frac{1}{3}$ of the counters are blue.

- $\frac{3}{8}$ of the counters are green.

The rest of the counters are yellow.

How many yellow counters are there?

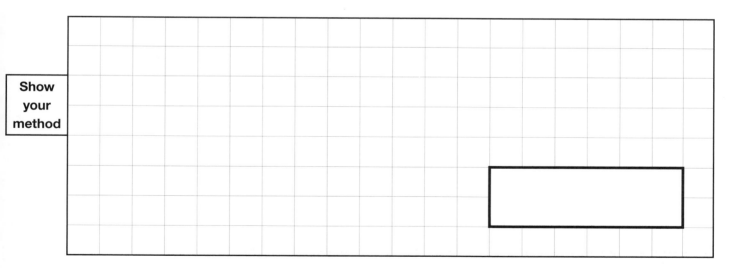

Show
your
method

11 878,421 − 319,875 =

Round each number in this calculation to the nearest hundred thousand to work out an estimated answer.

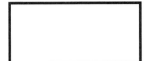

1 mark

12 For each number, give the value of the digit 8.

7,376,548

8,065,913

5,682,790

7,368,514

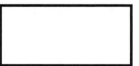

2 marks

13 An aeroplane is flying at a height of 8,000 m.

The outside temperature is −45°C.

Inside the aeroplane the temperature is 18°C.

What is the **difference** between the two temperatures?

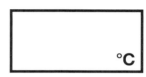

°C

1 mark

14 The population of a city is 275,386.

- 54,895 are aged 65 and over.

- 143,706 are aged 18 to 64.

How many are aged under 18?

Show your method

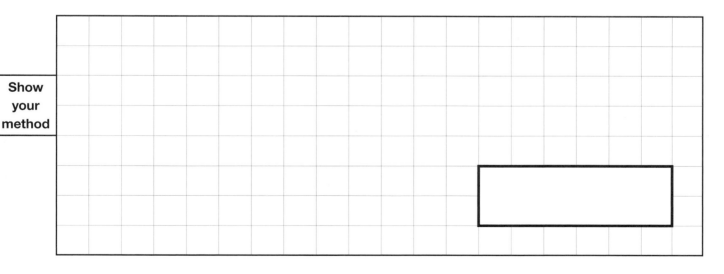

2 marks

15 Draw a line from a fraction to the common factor used to simplify it.

$\dfrac{24}{30}$ 3

$\dfrac{21}{30}$ 4

$\dfrac{28}{32}$ 5

$\dfrac{20}{25}$ 6

2 marks

16 These two triangles are the same shape but different sizes.

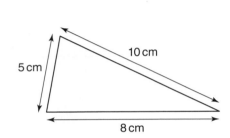 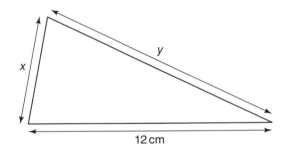

Work out the lengths of the sides x and y.

$x =$ [   ] cm

1 mark

$y =$ [   ] cm

1 mark

17 Write these lengths in order, **heaviest** first.

2.5 kg   200 g   2.05 kg   2,550 g   2.005 kg

☐   ☐   ☐   ☐   ☐

1 mark

18 Tick (✔) each box if the fact about the drawn shape is true.

	has at least 1 pair of parallel sides	has at least 1 pair of perpendicular sides
Right-angled triangle	☐	☐
Rectangle	☐	☐
Parallelogram	☐	☐

3 marks

19 Teachers asked 120 children where they would like to go on a school visit.

This pie chart shows where they chose to go.

School visit

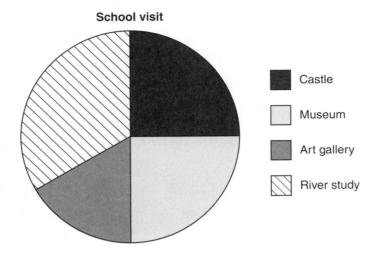

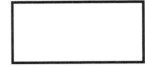
Castle

Museum

Art gallery

River study

> Estimate how many children chose to visit the castle.

40 children chose the river study.

> What size angle at the centre of the pie chart is needed to show the river study?

Half the children chose either the river study or the art gallery.

> How many children chose to visit the art gallery?

20 Abi sat 6 tests.

Her mean score was 45.

How many marks did Abi score **altogether**?

21 A formula to find the perimeter, P, of a rectangle is

$P = 2l + 2w$, where l = length and w = width

Work out the length of a rectangle that has a perimeter of 80 cm and a width of 10 cm.

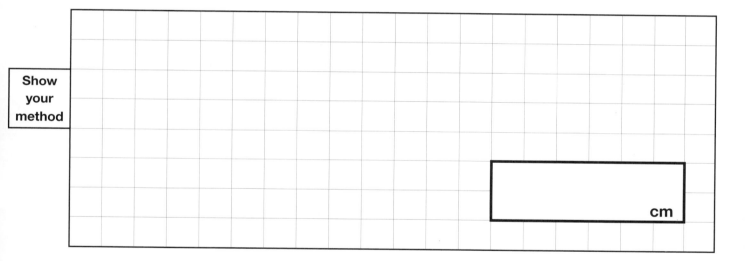

Show your method

cm

Key Stage 2

Maths

Paper 1: arithmetic

You **may not** use a calculator to answer any questions in this test paper.

Time:

You have **30 minutes** to complete this test paper.

Maximum mark	Actual mark
40	

First name	
Last name	

Date of birth	Day		Month		Year	

1   40 ÷ 5 =

2   828 − 102 =

3 $\dfrac{7}{8} - \dfrac{4}{8} =$

4	$\frac{1}{2}$ of 30 =		1 mark

5	888 + 1,000 =		1 mark

6	8,224 + 1,880 =		1 mark

7 765 ÷ 5 =

1 mark

8 0.6 × 100 =

1 mark

9 27,005 + 77,808 =

1 mark

10	$3^3 =$	
		1 mark

11	$4,088 \times 6 =$	
		1 mark

12	$12.45 - 8.49 =$	
		1 mark

13

$0.03 \times 6 =$

14

$\dfrac{1}{2} - \dfrac{1}{10} =$

15

$4 - 12 =$

16

325.8 + 4.67 =

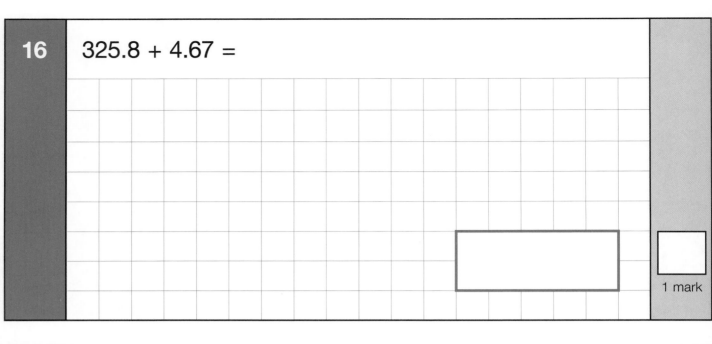

1 mark

17

80,000 – 8,000 =

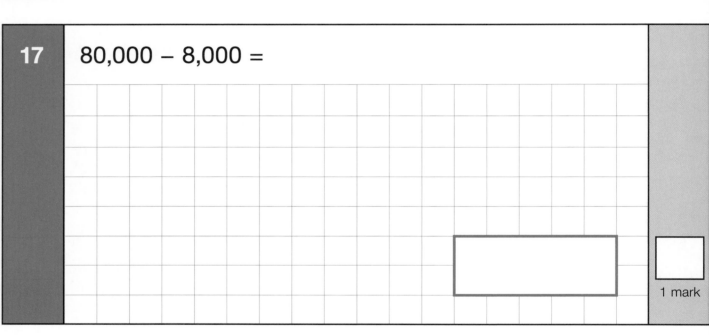

1 mark

18

$\frac{1}{10} \div 2 =$

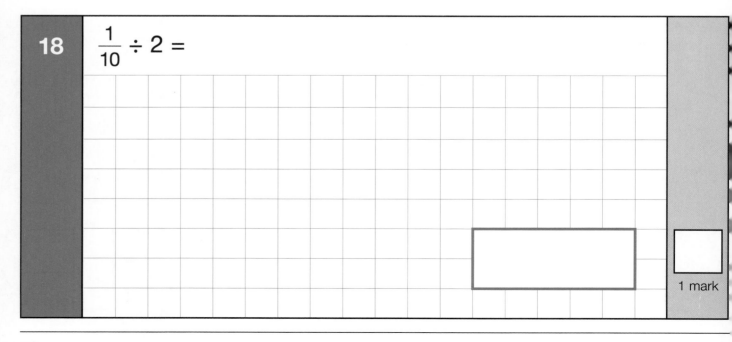

1 mark

19 690,360 – 251,069 =

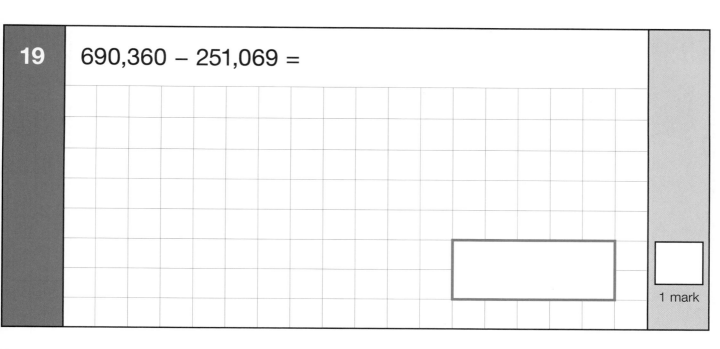

1 mark

20 23.9 + 4.76 + 0.74 =

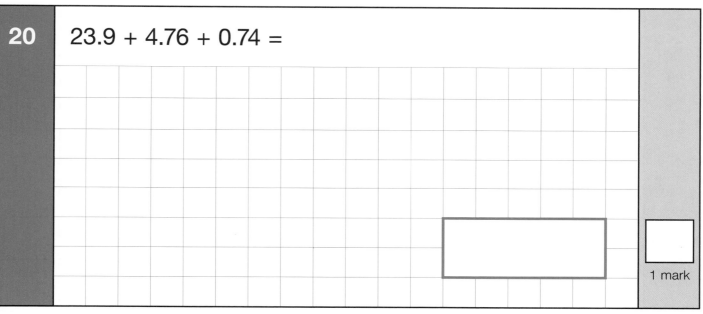

1 mark

21 $5\dfrac{3}{4} - \dfrac{3}{8} =$

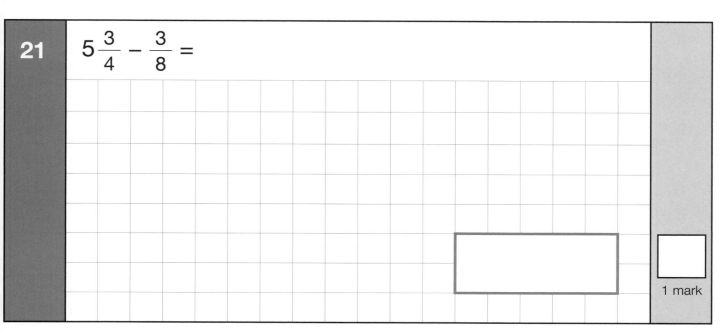

1 mark

22 20 × 30 × 40 =

1 mark

23 30% of 3,000 =

1 mark

24 75 ÷ 1,000 =

1 mark

25

654.23 − 40.8 =

26

Show your method

$$\begin{array}{r} 1\ 8\ 2 \\ \times\ 6\ 2 \\ \hline \end{array}$$

27

$100 \times 2\frac{1}{2} =$

1 mark

28

2 2 | 7 0 4

Show your method

2 marks

29

40 + 10 × 2 =

1 mark

30

Show your method

7 1 | 1 4 9 1

2 marks

31

$4\dfrac{2}{3} - 3\dfrac{3}{5} =$

1 mark

32

Show your method

```
      3 0 7 4
  ×       3 5
  _____
```

2 marks

33

4,000,000 – 400,000 =

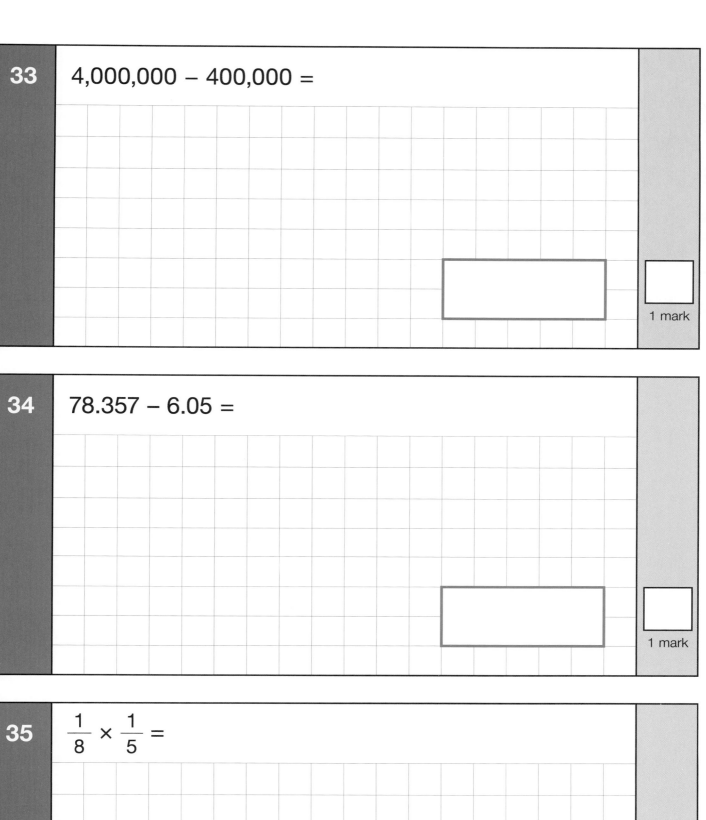

1 mark

34

78.357 – 6.05 =

1 mark

35

$\dfrac{1}{8} \times \dfrac{1}{5} =$

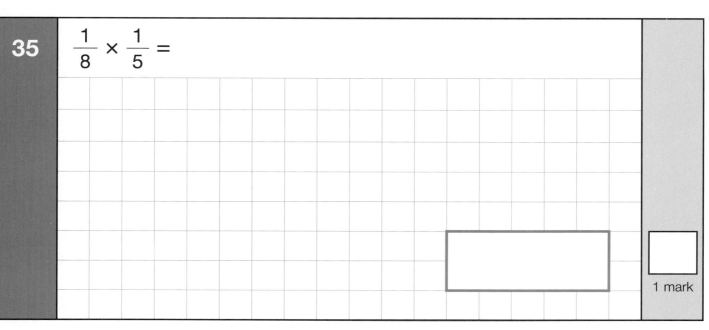

1 mark

36

$$\frac{2}{3} \div 2 =$$

1 mark

Key Stage 2

Maths

Paper 2: reasoning

You **may not** use a calculator to answer any questions in this test paper.

Time:

You have **40 minutes** to complete this test paper.

Maximum mark	Actual mark
35	....

First name	
Last name	

Date of birth	Day		Month		Year	

1 Tick (✔) the right angles in this shape.

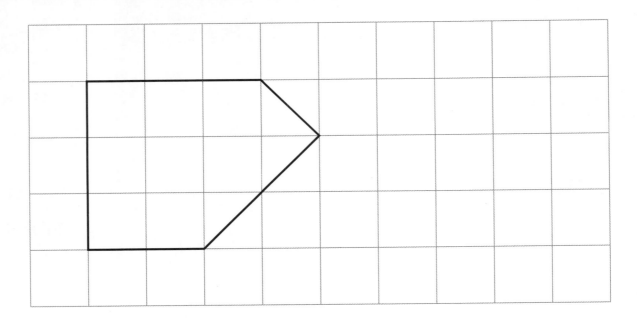

2 Here are some counters.

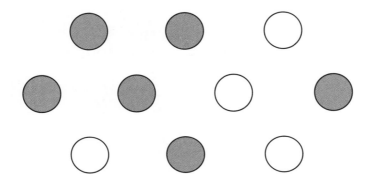

What fraction of the counters are grey?

3 Dev read 26 books in a school year.

He drew a graph to show how many books he read each term.

Complete the bar for Term 3.

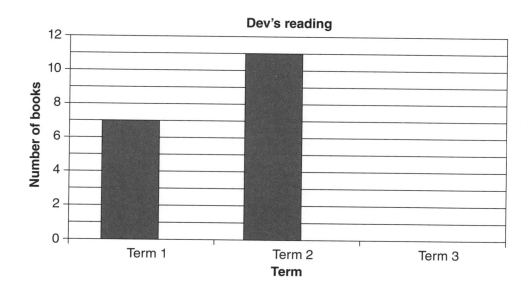

4 A train has 8 coaches.

Each coach has 72 seats.

The ticket collector says, 'I know 70 × 8 = 560'

What must he add to 560 to find how many seats there are in the train **altogether**?

5 Find the missing number.

$$64 \times 24 = (64 \times 20) + (64 \times \boxed{}) = 1{,}536$$

6 A square is drawn on an empty grid.

The coordinates of three vertices are marked.

> What are the coordinates of the fourth vertex?

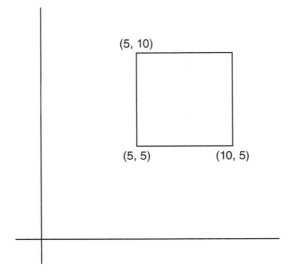

(5, 10)

(5, 5)   (10, 5)

$$\left(\underline{\hspace{1cm}} , \underline{\hspace{1cm}} \right)$$

1 mark

7 A shop has a special offer.

> Special offer!
>
> Buy 3 tins of soup and get 1 free

Obi pays for 12 tins of soup.

> How many tins does Obi get?

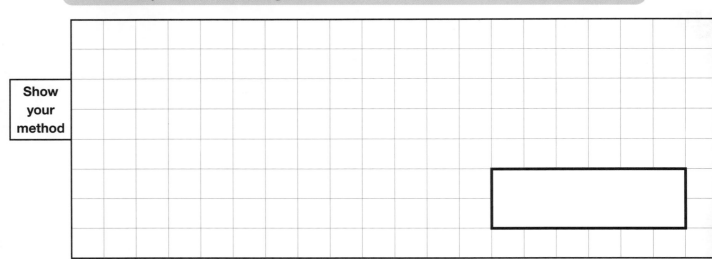

Show your method

2 marks

8 Max makes some concrete for a path.

For a path 8 metres long Max needs:

- 200 kg of cement

- 600 kg of sand

- 600 kg of stone

What weight of stone will he need for a path 20 metres long?

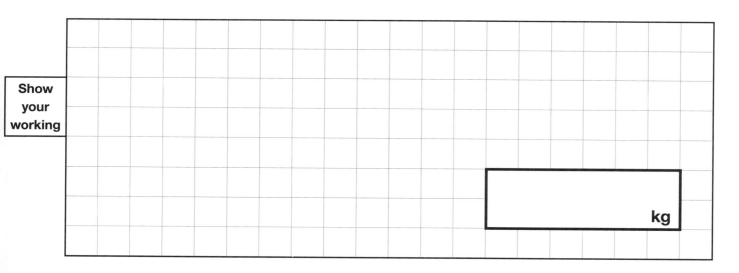

Show your working

kg

2 marks

9 Calculate the missing number.

$$56 \times 9 = 1{,}512 \div \boxed{}$$

1 mark

Calculate the missing number.

$$3 \times 8 = 72 \div 2 - \boxed{}$$

1 mark

Calculate the missing number.

$$56 + 64 = 3 \times 4 \times \boxed{}$$

1 mark

10 This table shows some approximate equivalent measures.

Metric	Imperial
2.5 cm	1 inch
30 cm	1 foot
90 cm	1 yard

Ula says, 'I am 5 feet 4 inches tall.'

How tall is she using **metric** measures?

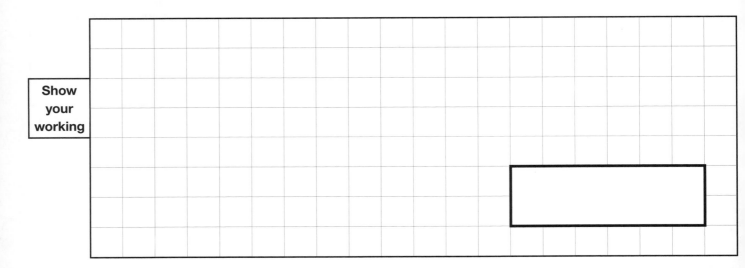

Show your working

2 marks

Here are some number cards.

| 4 | 4 | 5 | 5 | 6 | 6 |

Use the number cards to complete this equation.

Use each card only once.

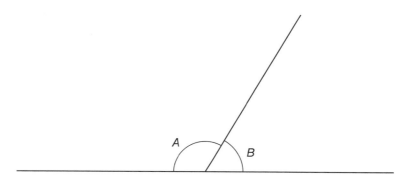

$\div\ 100 =$ ☐ . ☐☐

12

What is the **total** of angle *A* and angle *B*?

13 Here are two fair triangular spinners.

Each spinner is spun once and the numbers added to give a total.

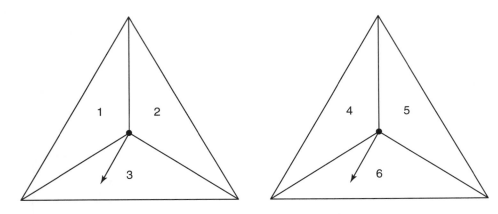

2 marks

14 This sequence decreases in equal steps.

Find the missing numbers.

 6   −3   −30

2 marks

68

15 This is a net.

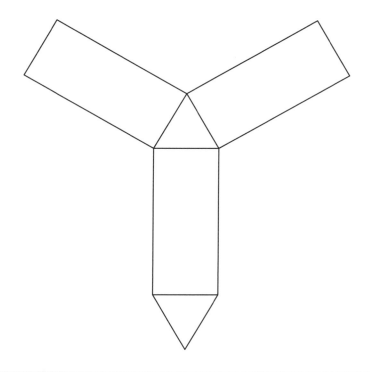

Name the 3-D shape.

1 mark

16 Josef is thinking of a six-digit number.

Josef's number has:

- Three hundred thousand

- Seven hundred

- Forty thousand

All the other digits are 6

Use these facts to complete the number.

1 mark

17 This table shows the temperatures in five cities.

City	London	Belfast	Manchester	Cardiff	Glasgow
Temperature	4°C	0°C	–3°C	–1°C	–5°C

What is the **difference** between the temperatures in Manchester and Cardiff?

°C

1 mark

What is the **difference** between the warmest and coldest temperatures?

°C

1 mark

18 Find the missing numerators in these equations.

$$\frac{3}{4} = \frac{\boxed{}}{24}$$

$$\frac{5}{6} = \frac{\boxed{}}{24}$$

$$\frac{3}{8} = \frac{\boxed{}}{24}$$

$$\frac{2}{3} = \frac{\boxed{}}{24}$$

2 marks

19 What could the missing numbers be?

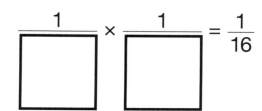

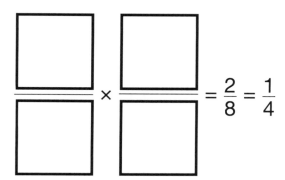

$$= \frac{2}{8} = \frac{1}{4}$$

20 Dev and Sam share £45

Dev takes half the amount Sam takes.

How much do they each take?

Dev takes

£

Sam takes

£

21 This rectangle has an area of 24 cm².

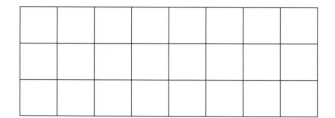

Write the lengths and widths of two different rectangles that also have the an area of 24 cm².

length [   ] cm and width [   ] cm

length [   ] cm and width [   ] cm

22 Angles *x* and *y* are equal.

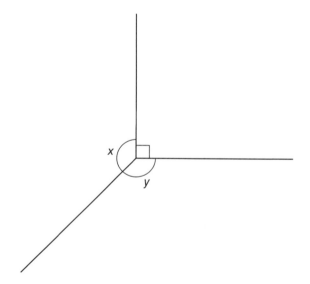

Calculate angle *x*.

X = [   ]°

23 Ben describes two shapes.

Name each shape.

My first shape has four
right angles and sides
of 10 cm and 5 cm.

_____

1 mark

My second shape has four
angles, two that are 120° and
two that are 60°, and sides
that are 10 cm and 5 cm.

_____

1 mark

Key Stage 2

Maths

Paper 3: reasoning

You **may not** use a calculator to answer any questions in this test paper.

Time:

You have **40 minutes** to complete this test paper.

Maximum mark	Actual mark
35	

First name	
Last name	

Date of birth	Day		Month		Year	

1 Here are some number cards:

| 3 | 4 | 5 | 6 | 7 |

Use each card once.

☐	☐	☐
+	☐	☐
6	0	1

2 marks

2 This is a rectangle.

Tick (✔) **two** correct statements.

The two bold lines are perpendicular. ☐

The bold and thin lines are perpendicular. ☐

The two bold lines are parallel. ☐

The bold and thin lines are parallel. ☐

2 marks

3 Dom sells computer games.

This pictogram shows the number of computer games he sold one week.

Computer Game Sales

⊙ stands for four computer games

Sunday	⊙ ⊙ ⊙ ⊙
Monday	⊙ ☾
Tuesday	⊙ ☾
Wednesday	⊙
Thursday	⊙ ⊙ ⊙
Friday	⊙ ⊙ ⊙ ☾
Saturday	⊙ ⊙ ⊙ ⊙

How many computer games did Dom sell on Friday and Saturday?

games

1 mark

How many more games did Dom sell on Sunday than on Monday?

games

1 mark

4 Tick (✔) all the shapes that have $\frac{2}{3}$ shaded.

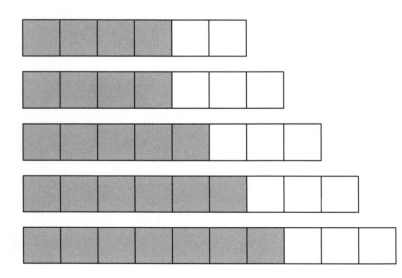

2 marks

76

5 Ned has a 10 kg bag of potatoes.

He uses 2.3 kg of the potatoes one day.

He uses 1,600 g of the potatoes on the next day.

What is the weight of potatoes left?

Show your working

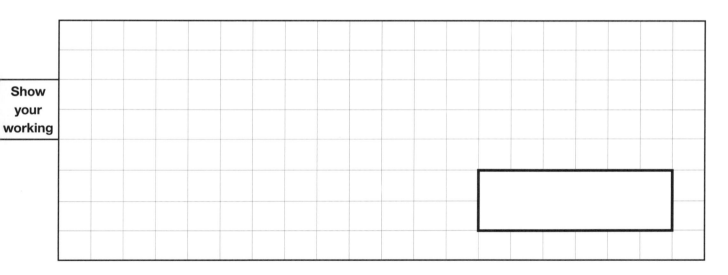

2 marks

6 Translate the shape 7 squares right and 3 squares down.

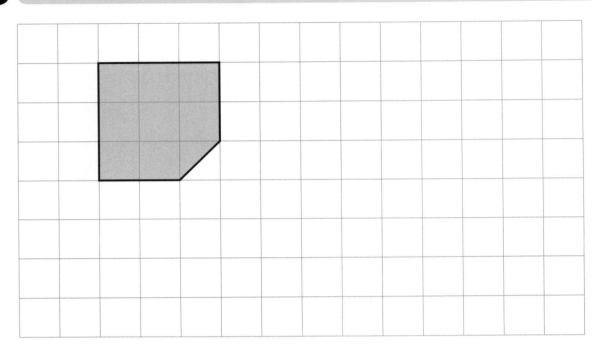

7 Write the year MMXXII in digits.

8 Circle the number that is both:

- a factor of 36

- a multiple of 12

9   18   24   36   72

9 | Round **196,704**

to the nearest ten

to the nearest thousand

to the nearest hundred thousand

2 marks

10 | Complete this table of equivalent fractions, decimals and percentages.

Fraction		Decimal		Percentage
$\frac{65}{100}$	=		=	
	=	0.8	=	
	=		=	7%

2 marks

11 Write the following as digits.

one million, thirty-seven thousand, six hundred and four

12 Here are three number cards.

| 1 | 2 | 3 |

Use each card to complete the missing numbers in these sentences.

Use each card only once.

5 ☐ is a prime number.

4 ☐ is a common multiple of 3 and 7

3 ☐ is a common factor of 62 and 93

13 Find the missing number.

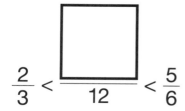

$$\frac{2}{3} < \frac{\boxed{}}{12} < \frac{5}{6}$$

1 mark

14 Tara thinks of a number, *n*

She adds 12 to the number and then multiplies the answer by 3

Tick (✔) the expression that shows this.

3*n* + 12

3(*n* + 12)

3 × 12 × *n*

36 + *n*

n(3 + 12)

1 mark

15 Measure the marked angle using a protractor.

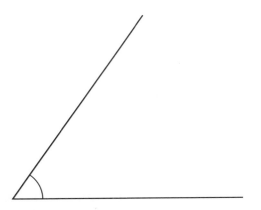

1 mark

16 Sam sat two maths tests.

These were his scores:

Paper 1: $\dfrac{14}{20}$

Paper 2: $\dfrac{18}{25}$

Change Sam's fraction scores to percentage scores.

Paper 1:  %

Paper 2:  %

2 marks

17 This pie chart shows the sports chosen by 80 children.

Here are some facts about the pie chart:

- 30 children chose tennis.

- $\frac{1}{4}$ of the children chose football.

- The same number of children chose gymnastics as chose rugby.

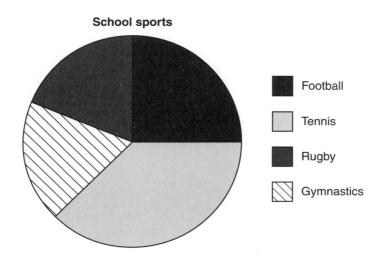

School sports

Football

Tennis

Rugby

Gymnastics

How many children chose rugby?

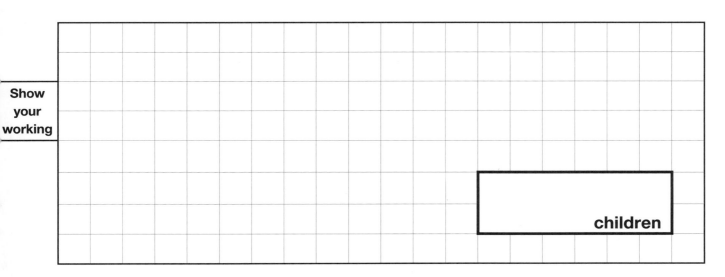

Show your working

children

2 marks

18 Tick (✔) the number with 7 as the hundredths digit.

6.497 ☐

64.97 ☐

649.7 ☐

6,497 ☐

64,970 ☐

649,700 ☐

1 mark

19 Work out the area of this triangle.

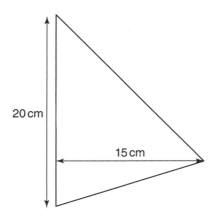

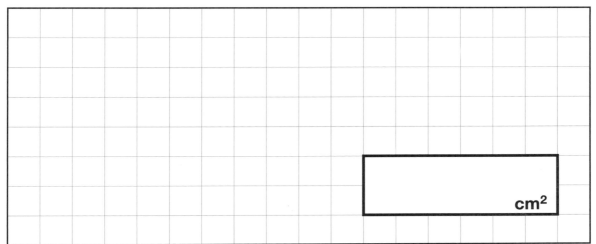

cm²

1 mark

Work out the length of this parallelogram.

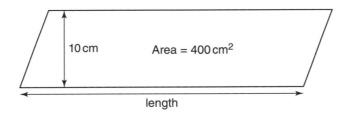

10 cm   Area = 400 cm²

length

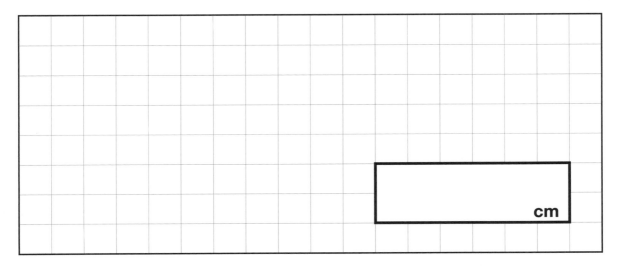

cm

1 mark

20 The dots, A to F, can be joined to make a straight line.

The dots are drawn at regular intervals.

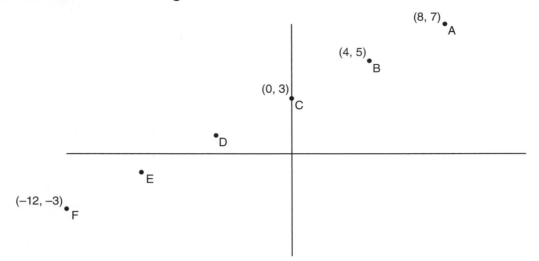

Some dots have coordinates.

What are the coordinates of dots D and E?

D = $\left(\underline{\quad},\underline{\quad}\right)$

E = $\left(\underline{\quad},\underline{\quad}\right)$

2 marks

21 Tickets to an amusement park cost £17.50 each.

There is a special offer. Eight tickets can be bought for £110.

How much cheaper is **each** ticket with the special offer?

Show your method

£

2 marks

Answers

Set A Paper 1

1.   215   **(1 mark)**

2.   630   **(1 mark)**

3.   1,334   **(1 mark)**

4. $\frac{4}{5}$ (Accept equivalent fractions. Accept 0.8)   **(1 mark)**

5.   8,999   **(1 mark)**

6.   3,434   **(1 mark)**

7.   1,821   **(1 mark)**

8.   0.81   **(1 mark)**

9.   77,930   **(1 mark)**

10. 25   **(1 mark)**

11. 3,115   **(1 mark)**

12. $\frac{7}{10}$ (Accept equivalent fractions)   **(1 mark)**

13. −5 (Do not accept 5−)   **(1 mark)**

14. $\frac{9}{10}$ (Accept equivalent fractions)   **(1 mark)**

15. $\frac{1}{6}$ (Accept equivalent fractions)   **(1 mark)**

16. $\frac{1}{8}$ (Accept equivalent fractions)   **(1 mark)**

17. 2.4   **(1 mark)**

18. 1,250   **(1 mark)**

19. 0   **(1 mark)**

20. 109,475   **(1 mark)**

21. 590,729   **(1 mark)**

22. 262.76   **(1 mark)**

23. 446.91   **(1 mark)**

24.

		2	3	4
	×		2	6
	1	4	0	4
	4	6	8	0
	6	0	8	4

(2 marks for correct answer. Award 1 mark for using long multiplication with no more than one error but wrong answer given. Do not award any marks if the 0 for multiplying by a ten is missing.)

25.

			2	4
2	3	5	5	2
		4	6	
			9	2
			9	2
				0

(2 marks for correct answer. Award 1 mark for using long division with no more than one error but wrong answer given.)

26. 3,075   **(1 mark)**

27. $1\frac{1}{12}$ (Accept equivalent fractions)   **(1 mark)**

28. 12.82   **(1 mark)**

29. 0.65   **(1 mark)**

30. 18.145   **(1 mark)**

31.

		5	7	3
	×		4	5
	2	8	6	5
2	2	9	2	0
2	5	7	8	5

(2 marks for correct answer. Award 1 mark for using long multiplication with no more than one error but wrong answer given. Do not award any marks if the 0 for multiplying by a ten is missing.)

32. $\frac{3}{20}$ (Accept equivalent fractions. Accept 0.15) **(1 mark)**

33.

			2	5
3	5	8	7	5
		7	0	
		1	7	5
		1	7	5
				0

(2 marks for correct answer. Award 1 mark for using long division with no more than one error but wrong answer given.)

34. 60 **(1 mark)**

35. $\frac{1}{15}$ **(1 mark)**

36. 50.993 **(1 mark)**

Set A Paper 2

1. 43, 67, 75, and 83 circled only.

(2 marks: 1 mark for three answers circled)

2. **(2 marks: 1 mark for a shape with five sides; 1 mark for a pair of parallel lines)**

3. $\frac{1}{2}$ (Accept $\frac{4}{8}$ or other equivalent fractions) **(1 mark)**

4. 33,758 and 34,758 ticked only.

(1 mark: 1 mark for both correct answers)

5.

5 **0** 4 **6**

+ **7** 5 **5** 4

1 2 6 0 0

(1 mark: all correct for 1 mark)

6. 64 cm **(1 mark)**

7. 8, 4 **(1 mark)**

8. 460,305 **(1 mark)**

9.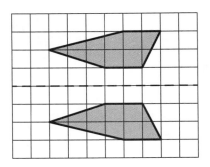

(Accept lines drawn to within 2 mm of vertices) **(1 mark)**

10. 15.4 pounds **(1 mark)**
10 kg **(1 mark)**

11. 48,100 **(1 mark)**
50,000 **(1 mark)**

12. 56.276 ticked only **(1 mark)**

13. 60 **(1 mark)**
66 **(1 mark)**

14. 41.25 **(1 mark)**

15. 40

(3 marks for correct answer. Award 1 mark for finding 40% of 460 = 184 or 1 mark for finding 60% of 240 = 144 or 1 mark for a correct subtraction of the answers even if the percentages are incorrect.)

16. 11 **(1 mark)**
45 **(1 mark)**

17. $\square$ = 12, $\triangle$ = 6

(2 marks for correct answer. Award 1 mark for $\square$ = 6, $\triangle$ = 12)

18. A **(1 mark)**
B **(1 mark)**
100 ml or 0.1 l **(1 mark)**

19. 4th shape ticked only. **(1 mark)**

20. 24 and 48 **(1 mark)**
15 and 30 **(1 mark)**
7 and 53 **(1 mark)**

21. 13°C (Accept +/– 1°C) **(1 mark)**
June and September **(1 mark)**

Set A Paper 3

1. 640 **(1 mark)**

2. 4 **(1 mark)**

3. 7.20 (Accept 7.20 am, 7.20 pm, 19.20, 20 past 7) **(1 mark)**

4.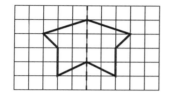

 (Accept lines drawn to within 2 mm of vertices. Ignore lines that are not straight.) **(1 mark)**

 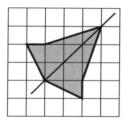

 (Accept lines drawn within 2 mm of the vertices.) **(1 mark)**

5. 217 − 83 = 134;
 134 + 350 = 484 minutes

 (2 marks for correct answer. Award 1 mark for correct working, but wrong answer given.)

6. £5.20 (Do not accept 5.2) **(1 mark)**

7. 30 cm **(1 mark)**
 Explanation should show that there are approximately 90 cm (3 × 30 cm) in 1 yard and 90 cm < 100 cm **(1 mark)**

8. 8°C **(1 mark)**

9. 2 and 29 (Accept answers in either order) **(1 mark)**
 41　43　47 **(1 mark)**

10. $(\frac{1}{4} \times 24) + (\frac{1}{3} \times 24) + (\frac{3}{8} \times 24) = 23$;
 6 + 8 + 9 = 23; 24 − 23 = 1

 (2 marks for correct answer. Award 1 mark for correct working, but wrong answer given.)

11. 600,000 (Do not accept 558,546) **(1 mark)**

12. 8 or eight units or eight ones
 8,000,000 or eight million
 80,000 or eighty thousand or eight ten thousands
 8,000 or eight thousand
 (2 marks: 2 marks for four correct answers, 1 mark for two or three correct answers)

13. 63°C **(1 mark)**

14. 275,386 − (54,895 + 143,706) = 76,785
 (2 marks for correct answer. Award 1 mark for correct working, but wrong answer given)

15.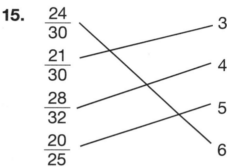

 (2 marks: 2 marks for four lines correctly drawn, 1 mark for two or three lines correctly drawn)

16. $x = 7.5$ cm **(1 mark)**
 $y = 15$ cm **(1 mark)**

17. 2,550 g　2.5 kg　2.05 kg
 2.005 kg　200 g (Accept units that have been converted correctly, e.g. 2,550 g　2,500 g　2,050 g 2005 g　200 g) **(1 mark)**

18. right-angled triangle　☐ ✓
 rectangle　✓ ✓
 parallelogram　✓ ☐
 (3 marks: 1 mark for each shape)

19. 30 (Accept +/− 1) **(1 mark)**
 120° **(1 mark)**
 20 **(1 mark)**

20. 270 **(1 mark)**

21. $80 = 2l + 2 \times 10$; $80 = 2l + 20$;

$60 = 2l$; $60 \div 2 = l = 30\,\text{cm}$

(2 marks for correct answer. Award 1 mark for correct working, but wrong answer given.)

Set B Paper 1

1. 8   **(1 mark)**

2. 726   **(1 mark)**

3. $\frac{3}{8}$ (Accept equivalent fractions. Accept 0.375)   **(1 mark)**

4. 15   **(1 mark)**

5. 1,888   **(1 mark)**

6. 10,104   **(1 mark)**

7. 153   **(1 mark)**

8. 60   **(1 mark)**

9. 104,813   **(1 mark)**

10. 27   **(1 mark)**

11. 24,528   **(1 mark)**

12. 3.96   **(1 mark)**

13. 0.18   **(1 mark)**

14. $\frac{2}{5}$ (Accept $\frac{4}{10}$ and other equivalent fractions. Accept 0.4)   **(1 mark)**

15. −8 (Do not accept 8−)   **(1 mark)**

16. 330.47   **(1 mark)**

17. 72,000   **(1 mark)**

18. $\frac{1}{20}$ (Accept equivalent fractions)   **(1 mark)**

19. 439,291   **(1 mark)**

20. 29.4   **(1 mark)**

21. $5\frac{3}{8}$ (Accept equivalent fractions. Accept $\frac{43}{8}$)   **(1 mark)**

22. 24,000   **(1 mark)**

23. 900   **(1 mark)**

24. 0.075   **(1 mark)**

25. 613.43   **(1 mark)**

26.

```
          1  8  2
    ×        6  2
          3  6  4
    1  0  9  2  0
    1  1  2  8  4
```

(2 marks for correct answer. Award 1 mark for using long multiplication with no more than one error but wrong answer given. Do not award any marks if the 0 for multiplying by a ten is missing.)

27. 250   **(1 mark)**

28.

```
               3  2
    2  2 | 7  0  4
           6  6
              4  4
              4  4
                 0
```

(2 marks for correct answer. Award 1 mark for using long division with no more than one error but wrong answer given.)

29. 60   **(1 mark)**

30.

```
                  2  1
    7  1 | 1  4  9  1
           1  4  2
                 7  1
                 7  1
                    0
```

(2 marks for correct answer. Award 1 mark for using long division with no more than one error but wrong answer given.)

31. $1\frac{1}{15}$ (Accept equivalent fractions)   **(1 mark)**

32.

```
             3  0  7  4
    ×           3  5
       1  5  3  7  0
       9  2  2  2  0
    1  0  7  5  9  0
```

(2 marks for correct answer. Award 1 mark for using long multiplication with no more than one error but wrong answer given. Do not award any marks if the 0 for multiplying by a ten is missing.)

33. 3,600,000   **(1 mark)**

34. 72.307   **(1 mark)**

35. $\frac{1}{40}$ (Accept equivalent fractions)

(1 mark)

36. $\frac{1}{3}$ (Accept equivalent fractions)

(1 mark)

Set B Paper 2

1.

(1 mark: all three right angles needed for 1 mark)

2. $\frac{3}{5}$ (Accept equivalent fractions, e.g. $\frac{6}{10}$, decimal, 0.6, and percentage, 60%) **(1 mark)**

3. A bar or line drawn to show 8

(1 mark)

4. 16 or 2 × 8 **(1 mark)**

5. 4 **(1 mark)**

6. (10, 10) **(1 mark)**

7. 12 ÷ 3 = 4; 12 + 4 = 16 tins

(2 marks for correct answer. Award 1 mark for correct working, but wrong answer given)

8. 20 ÷ 8 = 2.5; 600 × 2.5 = 1500 kg

(2 marks for correct answer. Award 1 mark for correct working, but wrong answer given)

9. 3 **(1 mark)**

12 **(1 mark)**

10 **(1 mark)**

10. 30 × 5 = 150; 2.5 × 4 = 10;

150 + 10 = 160 cm

(2 marks for correct answer. Award 1 mark for correct working, but wrong answer given)

11. Accept any correct answer, e.g.

456 ÷ 100 = 4.56; 465 ÷ 100 = 4.65;

546 ÷ 100 = 5.46; 564 ÷ 100 = 5.64;

645 ÷ 100 = 6.45; 654 ÷ 100 = 6.54

(1 mark)

12. 180° **(1 mark)**

13. 5   6   7   8   9

(2 marks: 2 marks for five correct answers, 1 mark for three or four correct answers)

14. −12   −21

(2 marks: 1 mark for each correct answer)

15. triangular prism **(1 mark)**

16. 346,766 **(1 mark)**

17. 2°C **(1 mark)**

9°C **(1 mark)**

18. $\frac{3}{4}$ = $\frac{18}{24}$

$\frac{3}{8}$ = $\frac{9}{24}$

$\frac{5}{6}$ = $\frac{20}{24}$

$\frac{2}{3}$ = $\frac{16}{24}$

(2 marks: 2 marks for four correct answers, 1 mark for two or three correct answers)

19. Accept $\frac{1}{2} \times \frac{1}{8}$ or $\frac{1}{8} \times \frac{1}{2}$

or $\frac{1}{4} \times \frac{1}{4}$ or $\frac{1}{1} \times \frac{1}{16}$ **(1 mark)**

$\frac{1}{2} \times \frac{2}{4}$ or $\frac{1}{1} \times \frac{2}{8}$ (Accept for either calculation numerators or denominators reversed) **(1 mark)**

20. Dev takes £15

Sam takes £30 **(1 mark)**

21. Possible answers are:

length   24 cm   width   1 cm

length   12 cm   width   2 cm

length   6 cm   width   4 cm

(Accept lengths and widths reversed. Accept fractions and decimals if correct, e.g. 48 cm × 0.5 cm. Do not accept length 3 cm width 8 cm)

(2 marks: 1 mark for each pair of correct answers)

22. 135° **(1 mark)**

23. rectangle (Accept oblong) **(1 mark)**
parallelogram **(1 mark)**

Set B Paper 3

1. Possible answers – 567 + 34,
534 + 37, 537 + 64, 534 + 67
**(2 marks: 1 mark for correct placing of
7 and 4 in the units column)**

2. 2nd and 3rd boxes ticked only.
**(2 marks: 1 mark for each correct
box ticked)**

3. 29 games **(1 mark)**
10 games **(1 mark)**

4. 1st and 4th shapes ticked only.
**(2 marks: 1 mark for each correct
box ticked)**

5. 10 – (2.3 + 1.6) = 6.1 kg or 10,000 –
(2,300 + 1,600) = 6,100 g (Accept 6.1 kg
or 6100 g. Units must be correct, e.g.
do not accept 6.1 g or 6,100 kg. Accept
6,100 or 6.1 without units.)
**(2 marks for correct answer. Award
1 mark for correct working, but wrong
answer given.)**

6.

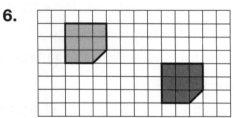

**(2 marks: 2 marks for drawing as
shown; 1 mark for correctly orientated
and sized shape translated 7 units
right or 3 units down)**

7. 2,022 **(1 mark)**

8. 36 circled only **(1 mark)**

9. 196,700
197,000
200,000
**(2 marks: 2 marks for three correct
1 mark for two correct)**

10.

Fraction		Decimal		Percentage
$\frac{65}{100}$	=	0.65	=	65%
$\frac{4}{5}$ or equivalent	=	0.8	=	80%
$\frac{7}{100}$	=	0.07	=	7%

**(2 marks: 2 marks for six correct
answers, 1 mark for four or five
correct answers)**

11. 1,037,604 (Accept misplaced
commas) **(1 mark)**

12. 53
42
31
**(2 marks: 2 marks for three correct
answers, 1 mark for two correct
answers)**

13. 9 **(1 mark)**

14. 2nd box ticked only **(1 mark)**

15. 55° (Accept angles within 2°) **(1 mark)**

16. Paper 1 70%
Paper 2 72% **(2 marks)**

17. $\frac{80 - (\frac{1}{4} \times 80 + 30)}{2}$ = 15 children
**(2 marks for correct answer. Award
1 mark for correct working, but wrong
answer given)**

18. 2nd box ticked only **(1 mark)**

19. 150 cm² **(1 mark)**
40 cm **(1 mark)**

20. D (–4, 1)
E (–8, –1)
(2 marks: 1 mark for each coordinate)

21. £17.50 – (£110 ÷ 8) = £17.50 – £13.75
= £3.75
**(2 marks for correct answer. Award
1 mark for correct working, but wrong
answer given)**

KS2 Success

Age 7-11

Science

Tests

Thomas Finch

Contents

(pull-out section at the back of the book)

Biology

- You have 25 minutes to complete this test.

1 Plant structure

a Label the diagram of the plant.

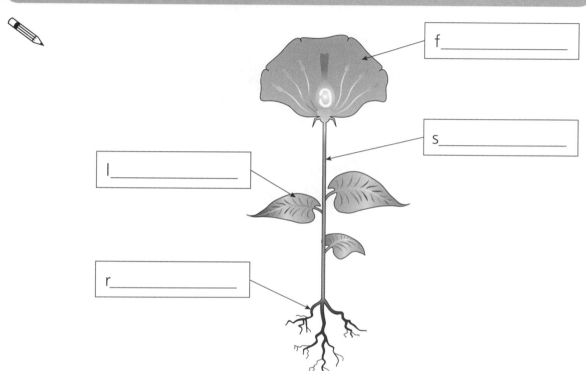

f_____

s_____

l_____

r_____

1 mark

b Draw a line to match each part of the flower with its function.

Stamen	The female part where seeds are made
Nectaries	Where nectar is made
Petal	The male part where pollen is made
Carpel	Attracts insects to the flower
Sepals	Protect the flower while it is a bud

3 marks

3

2 Teeth

a Bob is enjoying his tea. He knows that different teeth have different purposes when eating.

Explain the job of each type of tooth listed below.

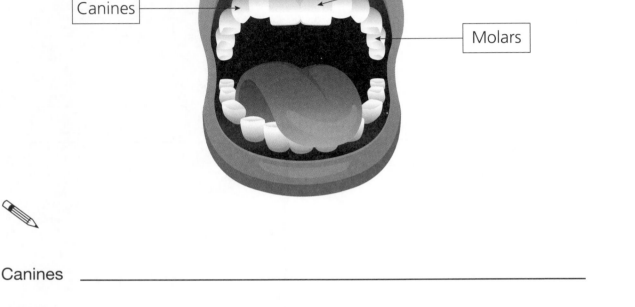

Canines _____

Incisors _____

Molars _____

3 marks

b Bob knows that he needs to keep his teeth healthy.

Suggest **TWO** things Bob must do to keep his teeth healthy.

1._____

_____

2._____

_____

2 marks

3 Animal adaptations

a Animals have adapted to suit their environments over many years.

Draw a line to match each animal with its environment.

1 mark

b Choose **ONE** of the animals above and give **ONE** way it has adapted to live in its environment.

Animal: _____

How has it adapted? _____

_____

1 mark

5

4 Genetics

a This picture shows some dogs.

Give **THREE** ways in which the dogs show variation.

1. _____

2. _____

3. _____

3 marks

b Children are not usually identical to their parents.

Name **TWO** ways that show that children are not identical to their parents.

1. _____

2. _____

2 marks

5 The heart

a Identify the different parts of the circulatory system indicated in the diagram below.

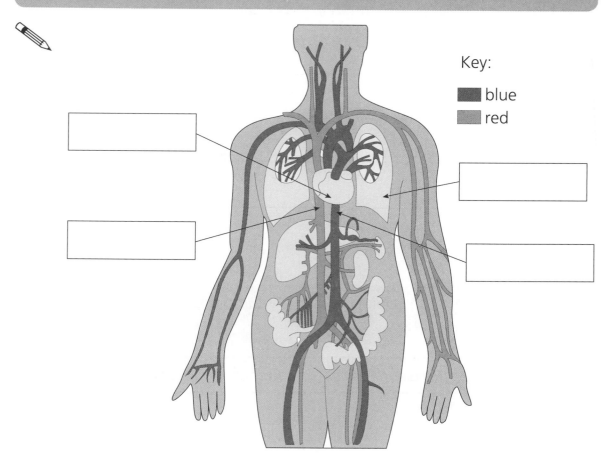

Key:
■ blue
■ red

3 marks

b Draw a line to match each part of the circulatory system with its function.

Arteries		Tubes that carry blood to the heart
Veins		Carries oxygen around the body
Blood		Pumps blood around the body
Heart		Tubes that carry blood away from the heart

2 marks

6 The human skeleton

All humans have a bony skeleton.

Give **TWO** reasons why a skeleton is important.

1. _____

_____

2. _____

_____

2 marks

Use the words in the box below to identify the different parts of the skeleton.

| Cranium (skull) | Fibula | Ribs | Femur | Humerus | Tibia |

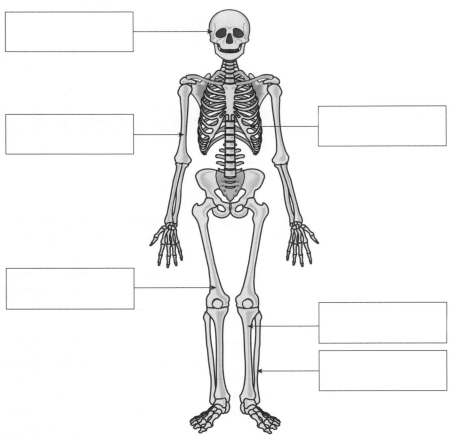

2 marks

Total _____/25 marks

8

Biology

- You have 25 minutes to complete this test.

1 Plant growth

a Plants need different things to live, including water.

> Explain why plants need water.

_____

_____ 1 mark

b Where does water enter the plant?

_____

_____ 1 mark

c. How does water get to the leaves and flowers?

_____

_____ 1 mark

9

2 Healthy lifestyles

a These people answered a survey on their lifestyles.

	Smoker	Healthy diet	Exercise
Ron	Yes	No	No
Kuba	No	Yes	No
Paul	Yes	Yes	Yes
Glen	No	Yes	Yes

Which person has the healthiest lifestyle?

_____
1 mark

b Why is smoking bad for smokers' lungs?

_____

_____
1 mark

c Explain why it is important to have a healthy lifestyle.

_____

_____
1 mark

3 Playing football

a Some children are playing football. Before they start playing, the children measure their pulses.

What does the pulse measure?

✏ _____

1 mark

b After the children have been playing for 15 minutes, they measure their pulses again.

What will they notice?

✏ _____

1 mark

c The children need to increase their breathing while doing exercise.

Why is it important to do this?

✏ _____

_____

_____

2 marks

4 Food chains

a Mia is working on her vegetable patch and has observed the following:

Slugs eat the cabbages.
Thrushes eat the slugs.

Show this on a food chain.

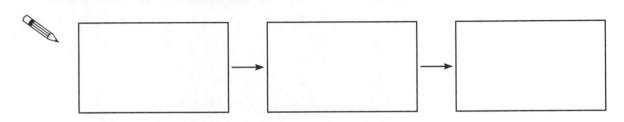

1 mark

b Match the follow things with the correct description.

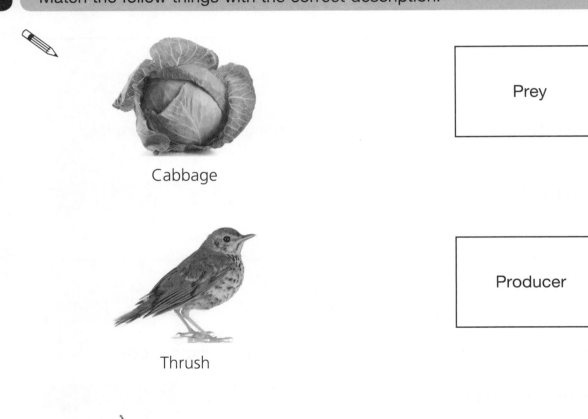

Cabbage

Thrush

Slug

Prey

Producer

Predator

3 marks

5 Digestion

a The digestive system is important to make sure we get the nutrients we need.

Write a number from 1 to 4 in each box to order these stages in the digestive system from start to finish.

☐ Excess water is absorbed back into the body in the large intestine.

☐ Digested food is absorbed into the bloodstream through the small intestine.

☐ Any undigested food passes out when we go to the toilet.

☐ Food is eaten, then digested in the mouth, stomach and small intestine.

2 marks

b Tick the name of the tube in which chewed food passes from the mouth to the stomach.

Small intestine ☐

Large intestine ☐

Oesophagus ☐

Rectum ☐

1 mark

6 Animals and their environments

a Animals have changed over millions of years.

Write down **ONE** feature of a polar bear that helps it in its environment.

_____

1 mark

b How does this help the polar bear in its environment?

_____

_____

1 mark

c Giraffes have developed long necks over time.

Give **TWO** advantages to the giraffe of having a long neck.

1. _____

_____

_____

2. _____

_____

_____

2 marks

d Over time the polar bears' environment has started to melt away.

How is this affecting polar bears?

_____

_____

_____

2 marks

Total _____ /23 marks

Biology

- You have 25 minutes to complete this test.

1 Plants

a Alice is planning an investigation on plants. She has set up three different plants around the room in different places.

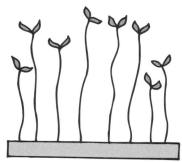

1. Next to the window

2. Inside a cupboard

3. Inside a plastic bag in the middle of the room

Alice waters each plant once a day.

> What is plant 2 missing in order to grow well?

_____

_____

1 mark

b > Name all **THREE** things that plants need to survive.

1. _____

2. _____

3. _____

3 marks

2 Muscles

a Humans have muscles throughout their bodies.
A group of children are getting ready for a PE lesson.

> Why do the children need to warm up and stretch their muscles before exercising?

_____

_____

1 mark

b The biceps muscle in the picture below is currently relaxed.

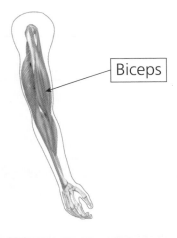

Biceps

> Explain what happens when this muscle is contracted.

_____

_____

_____

2 marks

3 Life cycles of animals

a Explain the difference between vertebrate and invertebrate animals.

_____

_____

1 mark

b Sort the following animals into the correct columns in the table.

| Mammals | Birds | Spiders | Insects |

Vertebrate	Invertebrate

2 marks

c Draw the life cycle of a penguin.

1 mark

4 Life cycles of plants

a Plants need to spread their seeds in order to make new plants.

Order the events in this process from 1 to 3.

☐ | Seeds are scattered by an animal or the wind.

☐ | Pollen is blown by the wind or carried by insects from one plant to another.

☐ | Pollen reaches the carpel of the new flower and travels to the ovary. It then fertilises ovules to make seed.

2 marks

b Identify the name of each event in the process.

(i) Seeds are scattered by an animal or the wind.

_____

1 mark

(ii) Pollen is blown by the wind or carried by insects from one plant to another.

_____

1 mark

(iii) Pollen reaches the carpel of the new flower and travels to the ovary. It then fertilises ovules to make seed.

_____

1 mark

c Describe the function of these parts of the plant.

Petal _____

Stamen _____

Carpel _____

3 marks

d Explain what germination is.

_____

_____

_____

1 mark

e Tick the part of the plant that takes in water and nutrients.

Leaves ☐

Roots ☐

Stem ☐

Flower ☐

1 mark

5 Human life

A baby is breathing in his cot.

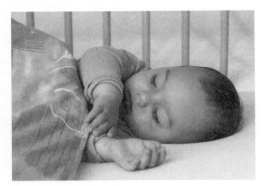

Tick the statements which show the baby is a living thing.

	Grows		Drinks milk
	Eats		Urinates
	Wears a hat		Cries
	Sits on the floor		Has a bath

2 marks

b   Complete the following life cycle of a human.

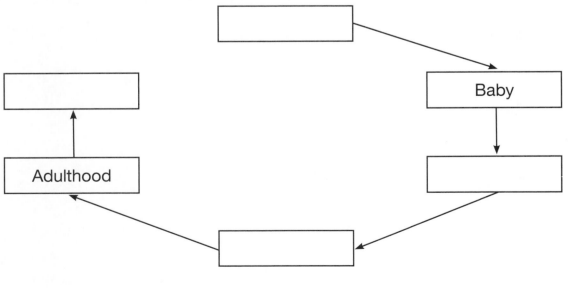

2 marks

Total _____/ 25 marks

Chemistry

- You have 25 minutes to complete this test.

1 Fire

a Hashim is making a fire. He lights a match to set fire to the wood.

What **THREE** things are formed when the wood burns?

1. _____

2. _____

3. _____ 1 mark

b What kind of material change is this?

| Irreversible | Reversible | Evaporating | Melting |

_____ 1 mark

2 Fossils

a This is a fossil of an animal from millions of years ago.

What material are fossils made of?

✎ _____

1 mark

b Write a number from 1 to 5 in each box to order the events that took place to make this fossil.

✎ ☐	Rock pushes the sediment down and water washes away the bones, leaving a space in the rock.
☐	Fossils are uncovered millions of years later.
☐	Sediment falls onto the skeleton of the animal.
☐	The animal dies and drops to the river bed.
☐	Water carries rock into the area where the animal was, creating a fossil.

3 marks

c Scientists can gather information from fossils.

Write down **TWO** things that scientists can learn by examining a fossil.

✎ 1. _____

2. _____

2 marks

3 Ice cubes

a Sid is enjoying a cold drink. As he drinks it, the ice cubes begin to melt.

Label each arrow with the name of the change that is happening.

One has been done for you.

| Melting | Evaporating | Freezing | Boiling | Condensing |

Melting

2 marks

b Name the type of change shown in the pictures above.

_____ 1 mark

c Explain what needs to happen in order for the ice cubes to melt.

_____

_____ 1 mark

4 Materials

a   What are the properties of these two materials?

Conductor _____

_____

Insulator _____

_____

2 marks

b   Give **ONE** important property of each of the following materials.

(i) Wood

_____

1 mark

(ii) Glass

_____

1 mark

24

(iii) Fabric

 _____

1 mark

c Explain the difference between transparent and opaque.

 _____

_____

_____

2 marks

d Copper is a good electrical conductor.

What does it mean if a material has a high value for electrical conductivity?

 _____

_____

1 mark

5 Keeping warm

a Charlotte is trying to keep warm.

Name **TWO** items of clothing she can wear that could keep her insulated.

1. _____

2. _____

2 marks

b Charlotte wants to improve the length of time her house stays warm.

Which of the following would work? Tick all that apply.

☐ roof insulation

☐ double glazing

☐ wooden roof

☐ single glazing

1 mark

c A radiator is a thermal conductor.

What does this mean?

_____

_____

1 mark

Total _____ / 24 marks

Chemistry

- You have 25 minutes to complete this test.

1 Jelly

a Freya is investigating different ways to make jelly.

She is going to make two lots of jelly. First, she dissolves jelly cubes in water. She uses hot water for one lot of jelly cubes and cold water for the other.

> Will the cubes dissolve more quickly in the hot water or the cold water?

_____

1 mark

b Freya notices that the jelly cubes don't look solid anymore.

> What has happened to the jelly cubes in the water?

_____

1 mark

c When making her jelly, Freya wants to speed up the process.

> What could Freya do to speed up the process that happens when she adds the jelly cubes to the water?
> Explain your answer.

_____

_____

_____

2 marks

2 Solids, liquids and gases

a Jane is looking at materials. She needs to categorise the materials she is investigating.

Sort the following materials into the correct columns in the table below.

Steam	Water	Wood	Glass	Sand	Helium	Milk

Solids	Liquids	Gases

3 marks

b Give **TWO** properties that a material has when it is in each of the states below.

Solid

 1. _____

2. _____

Liquid

 1. _____

2. _____

Gas

 1. _____

2. _____

3 marks

3 New bedroom

a Jed is planning a new bedroom. He has a variety of materials to use.

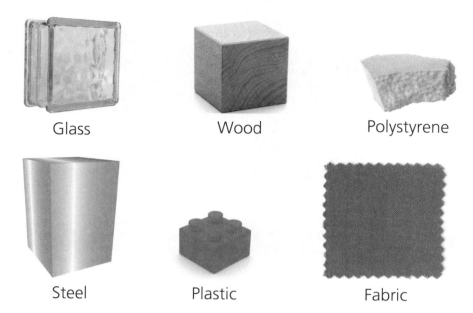

Glass   Wood   Polystyrene

Steel   Plastic   Fabric

Jed needs a material to put into the windows in his room.

Which material would be best to use?

_____

1 mark

b Explain why this is the best material for windows.

_____

_____

1 mark

c Which material is magnetic?

_____

1 mark

d Some fabrics are very absorbent.

What does this mean?

✏️ _____

_____

1 mark

e State what would need to be done to plastic to change its shape.

✏️ _____

_____

1 mark

f Plastic is a good electrical insulator.

What is the difference between an electrical insulator and an electrical conductor?

✏️

Electrical insulator _____

_____

Electrical conductor _____

_____

2 marks

4 Water cycle

The water cycle is an extremely important natural event.

Write a number from 1 to 4 in each box to order these events in the water cycle.

One has been done for you.

| 1 | Water evaporates into the air. |

| | Water falls as rain. |

| | Water vapour condenses into clouds. |

| | Water returns to the sea. |

2 marks

b What makes the water evaporate?

_____

_____

_____
2 marks

c When water vapour condenses, what is happening to the water?

_____

_____
1 mark

d Name **TWO** places water collects before it runs back to the sea.

1. _____

2. _____
2 marks

e In the water cycle, salty water from the sea eventually becomes rain water.

Why is rain water not salty?

_____

_____
1 mark

Total _____/25 marks

Chemistry

- You have 25 minutes to complete this test.

1 Rock and soil types

a Kelly has a number of rocks. She tries to scratch each rock with her fingernail. She can scratch off bits of the chalk but she cannot mark the other rocks.

Slate   Marble   Chalk   Granite

Which is the softest rock?

_____

1 mark

b Kelly pours water onto each rock to see what will happen. Some rocks are permeable and others are impermeable.

What do these terms mean?

Permeable

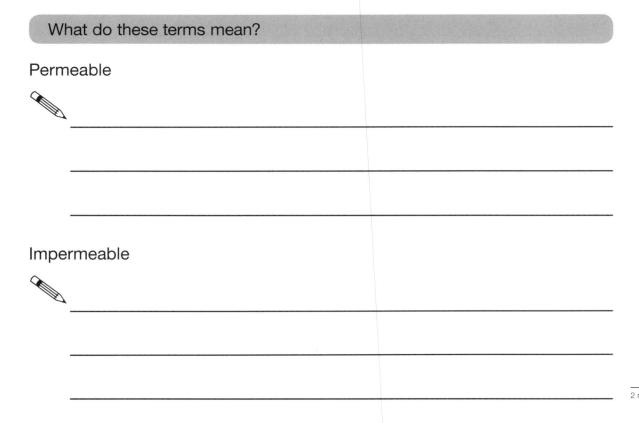

_____

_____

_____

Impermeable

_____

_____

_____

2 marks

c Kelly is planting some plants to grow over the summer. She knows that certain plants will grow better in different soils.

Name **TWO** things that soil is made up of.

1. _____

2. _____ 2 marks

d Kelly puts different soils into funnels. She pours the same amount of water into each funnel and observes how much water comes through after 10 minutes.

Water — Soil

A   B   C

Which soil let the most water through?

_____ 1 mark

e Funnel A: When dry, clay soil has very few air gaps.
Funnel B: When dry, sandy soil has lots of air gaps.
Funnel C: Chalky soil allows water to drain through it quickly.

Which funnel has each of the different soils in it?

Clay _____

Chalky _____

Sandy _____ 3 marks

2 Water temperature

a Jen is given four jars with water in them. She is told that some jars are warmer than others.

Fill in the table below with Jen's results.

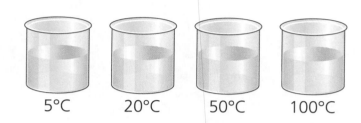

5°C   20°C   50°C   100°C

Jar	Temperature (°C)
Boiling water	
Warm water	
Water with ice	
Hot water	

2 marks

b Jen puts some ice into each of the jars.

In which jar will the ice melt the fastest?

_____

1 mark

c After the ice has melted Jen notices that the water level has increased from the original amount.

Why has this happened?

_____

_____

1 mark

d Jen takes the water from one jar and heats it in a pan on a hob.

Explain what will happen to the water.

_____

_____

_____ 2 marks

e What is the name of the process that makes steam change back to liquid water?

_____ 1 mark

f Jen puts another jar of water in the freezer.

At what temperature does water freeze?

_____ 1 mark

3 Changes in materials

a Sarah is making some toast.

Can Sarah turn her toast back into bread? Explain your answer.

_____

_____
2 marks

b What kind of change is this?

_____
1 mark

c Tick which of the following are reversible changes.

Melting chocolate ☐

Baking bread ☐

Frying an egg ☐
1 mark

(i) **Copy** the diagrams and add labelled arrows to show how ice, liquid water and steam are linked by reversible changes.

3 marks

(ii) Explain what your labelled diagram shows.

_____

_____

_____

_____

_____

2 marks

Total _____ /26 marks

Physics

- You have 25 minutes to complete this test.

1 Earth, Sun and Moon

a Joe is trying to find objects that show the Earth, Moon and Sun to scale for a project.

> Write under each object which one of Earth, Moon and Sun would fit best.

Grain of sand   Exercise ball   Tennis ball

_____   _____   _____

1 mark

b How often does the Moon orbit the Earth?

_____

_____

1 mark

2 Circuits

a Here is part of a series circuit.

(i) Finish drawing the circuit by including a closed switch and a bulb, using the correct symbols.

1 mark

(ii) Will the circuit work?

1 mark

b Will the lamp light in this circuit? Tick the correct answer box.

Yes ☐

No ☐

1 mark

c Will the motor work in this circuit? Tick the correct answer box.

Yes ☐

No ☐

1 mark

d Will the lamps light in this circuit? Tick the correct answer box.

Yes ☐

No ☐

1 mark

3 How we see

a Kamil is exploring how he can see different objects.

Using arrows, show how light travels so Kamil can see his scooter.

1 mark

b Give an example of a natural and an unnatural source of light.

Natural _____

Unnatural _____

2 marks

4 Friction

a Raaj has a toy car. He has been exploring how it travels on different surfaces and has noticed that it travels in different ways. He pushes the toy car and lets it go.

Put the following surfaces in order from the one on which the toy car travels the least distance to the one on which it travels the furthest.

Carpet   Long grass   Tiles

_____   _____   _____

Least   Furthest

1 mark

b Explain why the toy car will eventually stop on the surfaces.

_____

_____

_____

_____

2 marks

5 Magnets

Sort the following items into magnetic and not magnetic.

| Gold | Steel | Plastic | Iron | Wood | Copper |

Magnetic	Not magnetic

2 marks

b

Explain why these magnets will not be attracted to each other.

S   N   N   S

_____

_____

_____

2 marks

c

Complete the sentence below.

Sometimes magnets are not attracted to each other. In other words

they _____ each other.

1 mark

43

6 Making sounds

a Grace plucks the strings on the guitar and hears a sound.

> What makes the sound?

✎ _____

1 mark

b Grace can make sounds of different pitches.

> Complete the following sentences.

✎ Making a string shorter makes a sound with a _____ pitch.

Making a string longer makes a sound with a _____ pitch.

1 mark

c Grace plays a song for her friend.

> Explain how Grace can make a soft sound and a loud sound on her guitar.

✎ _____

_____

_____

_____

2 marks

Total _____/22 marks

Physics

- You have 25 minutes to complete the test.

1 Gravity

a Ted drops a parachute from a 5 metre height. He knows that gravity and air resistance are acting on it.

Draw arrows on the diagram below to show the directions of these two forces.

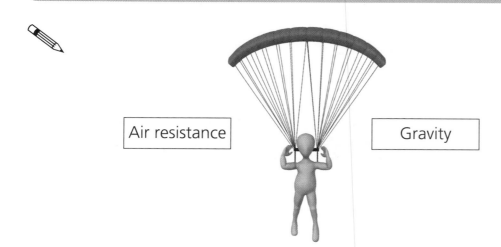

Air resistance

Gravity

2 marks

b Describe how the two forces act on the parachute.

Air resistance

_____

_____

Gravity

_____

_____

2 marks

c Ted has a second parachute. The second parachute is twice the size of the first.

Tick which parachute will fall more slowly.

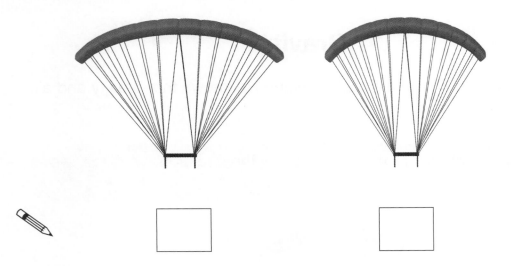

☐　　　　　　　☐

1 mark

d Why does your chosen parachute fall more slowly?
Link your answer to air resistance.

_____

_____

_____

_____

2 marks

e Ted investigates gravity further. He has two pieces of paper. One is screwed up into a ball, the other is flat.

Which piece of paper will hit the floor first when they are dropped at the same time from the same height? Explain your answer.

_____

_____

2 marks

2 Forces

a Jay is collecting water from a well.

What system is in place to help Jay get the bucket up and down the well?

_____

1 mark

b Name **ONE** other system that can be used to help people against forces.

_____

1 mark

c Complete the following sentence.

Gears consist of a system of _____ that allows a _____

turning force to have a _____ effect.

3 marks

3 Light and shadows

a Fred has a torch and is investigating how the position of the torch changes the shadow made against a block of wood.

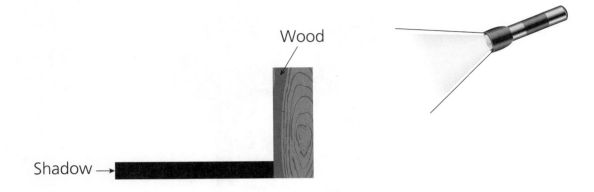

Wood

Shadow →

> What will happen to the length of the shadow if the torch is lowered?

_____

_____

1 mark

b Draw where the torch needs to be in order to create a shorter shadow than is shown in the diagram above.

1 mark

4 Planets

Put these planets in order from the closest to the furthest away from the Sun.

Jupiter

Neptune

Venus

Saturn

_____ _____ _____ _____

Closest   Furthest

2 marks

b Name the star at the centre of our solar system.

_____

1 mark

5 How we see things

a Ruby is trying to look at a bowl of fruit placed behind a wall. She is investigating the ways in which she can see it.

Draw where Ruby could place a mirror in order to see the bowl with the wall in the way.

1 mark

b Explain how Ruby can see the bowl of fruit using a mirror.

_____

_____

_____

1 mark

Total _____/21 marks

Physics

- You have 25 minutes to complete this test.

1 Day and night

a Kim is making a note of where the Sun is at different times of the day.
She comes up with three reasons for why the Sun moves throughout the day.

1. The Sun must orbit the Earth!

3. The Earth must orbit the Sun!

2. The Sun must move past the Earth and get covered up by the Moon at night!

Which of these statements is true?

_____

1 mark

b Explain how day and night occur in more detail.

_____

_____

_____

2 marks

51

c Kim watches the Moon each night. She notices that the Moon looks different each night and on some nights she can't see it.

On the diagram draw the Moon and how it moves in relation to the Sun and Earth.

1 mark

d Kim comes up with four statements from her investigations on the Sun, Moon and Earth.

Mark if each statement is true (T) or false (F).

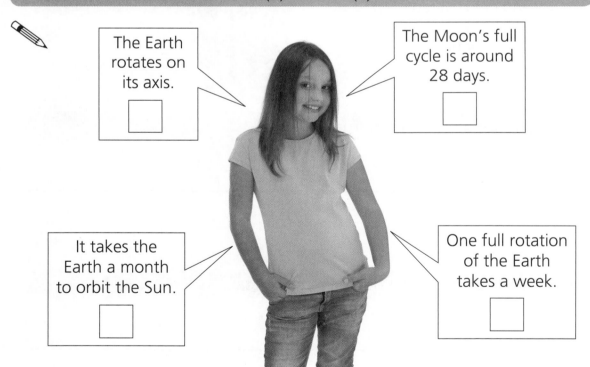

The Earth rotates on its axis.

The Moon's full cycle is around 28 days.

It takes the Earth a month to orbit the Sun.

One full rotation of the Earth takes a week.

3 marks

2 Electrical objects

Pryia is experimenting with some circuits. She is putting different objects in her circuits to see if the bulb will still light up.

(i) Put a tick in the correct box to indicate if the circuit will or will not work.

Iron bar

Will work ☐

Will not work ☐

_____
1 mark

(ii) Put a tick in the correct box to indicate if the circuit will or will not work.

Plastic tube

Will work ☐

Will not work ☐

_____
1 mark

b Pryia knows that there are electrical conductors and electrical insulators.

Explain what each of these are.

Conductor

_____

_____

Insulator

_____

_____

2 marks

c Pryia looks at some objects around her house. She organises them into two categories: runs on electricity and does not run on electricity.

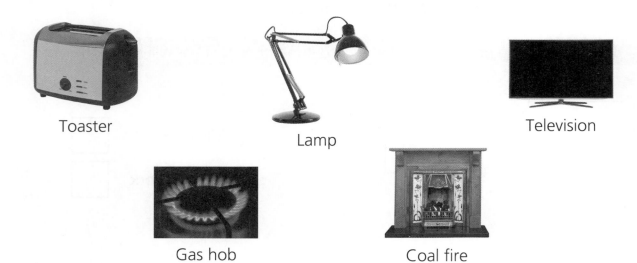

Toaster

Lamp

Television

Gas hob

Coal fire

Sort the items into these two categories.

Runs on electricity	Does not run on electricity

2 marks

3 Spinners

a Katie is preparing her spinners for an investigation into forces. She is trying to think of something that she can change in her experiment. She decides to change the number of paper clips attached to the bottom of the spinner.

> Write down **TWO** other changes she could have made.

🖉 1. _____

2. _____

2 marks

b Katie performs the investigation and drops each spinner from the same height.

> Which **TWO** main forces are acting on the spinner as it drops?

🖉 1. _____

2. _____

2 marks

c Katie creates a table to show her results.

Number of paper clips	Time (s)
1	5.0
2	4.1
3	2.9
4	2.5

Katie dropped each spinner three times. She then took an average of the results.

> Why does Katie need to drop each spinner three times and take an average?

🖉 _____

_____

1 mark

d Katie then creates a bar chart showing her results. Complete the bar chart.

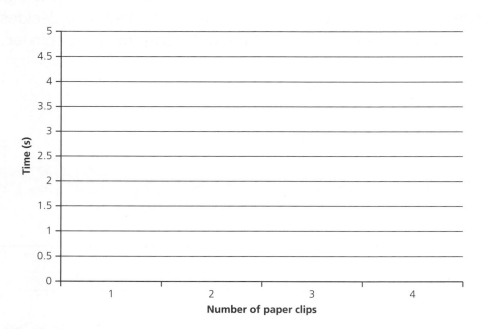

Time (s) axis: 5, 4.5, 4, 3.5, 3, 2.5, 2, 1.5, 1, 0.5, 0

Number of paper clips axis: 1, 2, 3, 4

3 marks

e Katie uses her graph to interpret the results.

Which spinner fell the slowest?

_____

1 mark

f Explain what would happen if there was a spinner with no paper clips.

_____

_____

_____

1 mark

Total _____/23 marks

Answers

Biology Test 1

1. a

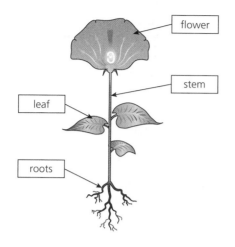

flower
stem
leaf
roots

(1 mark)

b

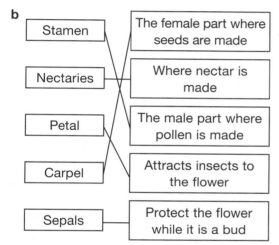

Stamen — The female part where seeds are made
Nectaries — Where nectar is made
Petal — The male part where pollen is made
Carpel — Attracts insects to the flower
Sepals — Protect the flower while it is a bud

(3 marks: 0 marks for one correct answer, 1 mark for two or three correct answers, 2 marks for four correct answers, 3 marks for five correct answers)

2. a Canines – used for tearing and ripping food
Incisors – help to bite off bits of food
Molars – help to crush and grind food **(3 marks)**

b Any two from: brush teeth twice a day; avoid sugary food and drinks; visit the dentist regularly **(2 marks)**

3. a

(1 mark)

b One of the following for one animal:

Giraffe – can consume and store water for long periods of time; long necks to feed and see predators from a distance; tough tongues to pull leaves off without being hurt by thorns

Penguin – layer of fat and thick skin to keep warm; huddle together to keep warm; waterproof feathers help them to swim in cold water

Camel – long eyelashes to keep sand out of their eyes; nostrils that can open and close; thick eyebrows to shade the eyes from the sun; store water in their hump

Or any other suitable answers. **(1 mark)**

4. a Any three from: different sizes; different shapes; different colours; different fur; different ears **(3 marks)**

b Any two from: different eye colour; different hair colour; different feet size; different heights **(2 marks)**

5. a

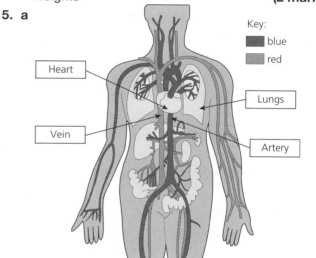

Key:
■ blue
■ red

Heart
Lungs
Vein
Artery

(3 marks: 1 mark for one or two correct answers, 2 marks for three correct answers, 3 marks for four correct answers)

b

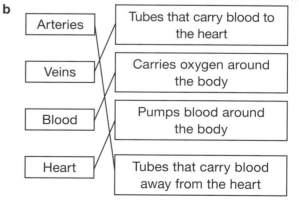

Arteries — Tubes that carry blood to the heart
Veins — Carries oxygen around the body
Blood — Pumps blood around the body
Heart — Tubes that carry blood away from the heart

(2 marks: 0 marks for one correct answer, 1 mark for two or three correct answers, 2 marks for four correct answers)

6. a Any two from: to protect important organs in the body; to support the body; to help the body move **(2 marks)**

b

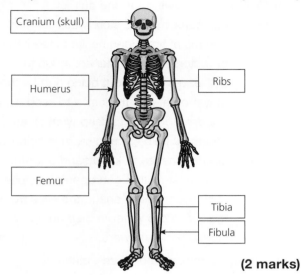

Cranium (skull)

Humerus

Ribs

Femur

Tibia

Fibula

(2 marks)

Biology Test 2

1. a Any one from: to have a strong stem and keep the plant healthy; so that the plant can make its own food. **(1 mark)**

b Water enters the plant through its roots. **(1 mark)**

c It is transported up the stem to the leaves and flowers. **(1 mark)**

2. a Glen **(1 mark)**

b Any one from: the smoker will struggle to breathe; the smoker may cough often; the smoker may get lung cancer; any other correct answer. **(1 mark)**

c To help your body and organs work properly. **(1 mark)**

3. a The heart rate **(1 mark)**

b The children's pulses increase **(1 mark)**

c It is important to increase breathing so more oxygen is moving around the body. **(1 mark)** Your muscles are working harder so they need more oxygen. **(1 mark)**

4. a

cabbage → slug → thrush

(1 mark)

b Cabbage – Producer
Slug – Prey
Thrush – Predator **(3 marks)**

5. a

3	Excess water is absorbed back into the body in the large intestine.
2	Digested food is absorbed into the bloodstream through the small intestine.
4	Any undigested food passes out when we go to the toilet.
1	Food is eaten, then digested in the mouth, stomach and small intestine.

(2 marks: 0 marks for one correct answer, 1 mark for two correct answers, 2 marks for four correct answers)

b Oesophagus **(1 mark)**

6. a Any one from: white fur; layer of fat and thick layer of fur; wide large paws **(1 mark)**

b Any one from: white fur helps the polar bear blend in with its surroundings; layers of fat and thick layers of fur keep the polar bear warm; wide paws help the polar bear walk on snow. **(1 mark)**

c 1. To see predators in the distance. **(1 mark)**
2. To reach food that is high in the trees. **(1 mark)**

d If the ice is melting it means the polar bears' habitat will slowly disappear, meaning polar bears may disappear one day. **(2 marks)**

Biology Test 3

1. a It is missing light **(1 mark)**

b light, water, air **(3 marks)**

2. a Any one from: so they are able to stretch more easily; to avoid pulling a muscle when exercising. **(1 mark)**

b When the biceps muscle contracts it will shorten and bring up the lower arm. **(2 marks)**

3. a Vertebrates have a backbone but invertebrates do not. **(1 mark)**

b

Vertebrate	Invertebrate
mammals birds	spiders insects

(2 marks: 1 mark for each correct column)

c

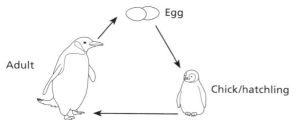

Adult → Egg → Chick/hatchling → Adult

(1 mark)

4. a

3	Seeds are scattered by an animal or the wind.
1	Pollen is blown by the wind or carried by insects from one plant to another.
2	Pollen reaches the carpel of the new flower and travels to the ovary. It then fertilises ovules to make seed.

(2 marks: 1 mark for one correct answer, 2 marks for three correct answers)

b (i) Dispersal **(1 mark)**

(ii) Pollination **(1 mark)**

(iii) Fertilisation **(1 mark)**

c Petal – bright to attract insects

Stamen – the male part of the plant that makes the pollen

Carpel – the female part of the plant where the seeds are made **(3 marks)**

d This is when a new plant starts to grow from the seed. **(1 mark)**

e Roots **(1 mark)**

5. a Grows; eats; cries; urinates; drinks milk

(2 marks: 1 mark for one to three correct answers, 2 marks for four or five correct answers)

b

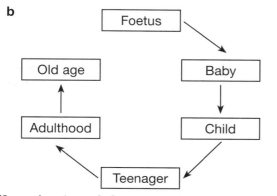

Foetus → Baby → Child → Teenager → Adulthood → Old age

(2 marks: 1 mark for one or two correct answers, 2 marks for three or four correct answers)

Chemistry Test 1

1. a Ash, smoke, gases **(1 mark)**

b Irreversible **(1 mark)**

2. a Rock **(1 mark)**

b

3	Rock pushes the sediment down and water washes away the bones, leaving a space in the rock.
5	Fossils are uncovered millions of years later.
2	Sediment falls onto the skeleton of the animal.
1	The animal dies and drops to the river bed.
4	Water carries the rock into the area where the animal was, creating a fossil.

(3 marks: 1 mark for one or two correct answers, 2 marks for two to four correct answers, 3 marks for five correct answers)

c Any two from: how long the animal lived; how things are related; how the animal lived; the environment that they lived in. **(2 marks)**

3. a

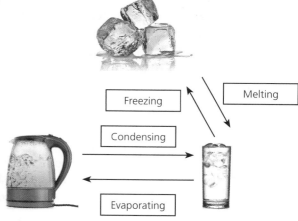

Freezing / Melting / Condensing / Evaporating

(2 marks: 1 mark for each pair of correct answers)

b Reversible **(1 mark)**

c They need to have heat applied to them. **(1 mark)**

4. a Conductor – a material that allows electricity to go through it.

Insulator – a material that does not allow electricity to go through it; keeps something warm or cold **(2 marks)**

b (i) Wood – Strong

(ii) Glass – Transparent, brittle, electrical insulator

(iii) Fabric – Light, flexible

(3 marks: 1 mark for one correct answer for each material)

c Any two from: you can see through materials that are transparent; you cannot see through materials that are opaque; light can travel through transparent materials, but cannot travel through opaque materials.

(2 marks: 1 mark for each correct definition)

d Electricity travels through it easily **(1 mark)**

5. a Any two from: jumper; coat; socks; scarf; gloves; hat **(2 marks)**

b roof insulation, double glazing **(1 mark)**

c It allows heat energy out into the room. **(1 mark)**

Chemistry Test 2

1. a Hot water **(1 mark)**

b They have dissolved. **(1 mark)**

c She could use hotter water and stir the jelly. **(1 mark)**

This will make the jelly cubes dissolve more quickly. **(1 mark)**

2. a Solids – wood, glass, sand

Liquids – water, milk

Gases – steam, helium

(3 marks: 1 mark for two or three correct answers, 2 marks for four or five correct answers, 3 marks for six or seven correct answers)

b Solid   Stays in one place and can be held; keeps its shape; can be cut or shaped

Liquid Can flow and be poured; changes shape to fit its container

Gas   Does not keep its shape; fills the space it is in; can be squashed

(3 marks: 1 mark for two correct statements for each state)

3. a Glass **(1 mark)**

b Glass is the best material for windows because it is transparent. **(1 mark)**

c Steel **(1 mark)**

d It means that fabric holds water when it gets wet. **(1 mark)**

e Plastic needs to be heated, then it can be moulded. **(1 mark)**

f Electrical insulator means that electricity cannot pass through a material. Electrical conductor means that electricity can pass through a material. **(2 marks)**

4. a

1	Water evaporates into the air.
3	Water falls as rain.
2	Water vapour condenses into clouds.
4	Water returns to the sea.

(2 marks: 1 mark for one or two correct answers, 2 marks for three or four correct answers)

b The sun heats the water up. **(1 mark)**

This creates water vapour. **(1 mark)**

c It is changing from vapour to liquid. **(1 mark)**

d 1. Lakes

2. Rivers **(2 marks)**

e Any one from: water evaporates but salt does not; only water evaporates. **(1 mark)**

Chemistry Test 3

1. a Chalk **(1 mark)**

b Permeable – A permeable rock allows water to soak through it

Impermeable – An impermeable rock does not allow water to soak through it. **(2 marks)**

c Any two from: tiny pieces of rock; tiny pieces of dead plants; tiny pieces of dead animal; tiny pieces of air; tiny drops of water **(2 marks)**

d B **(1 mark)**

e Clay – C

Chalky – B

Sandy – A

(3 marks: 1 mark for each correct answer)

2. a Boiling water – 100°C

Warm water – 20°C

Water with ice – 5°C

Hot water – 50°C

(2 marks: 1 mark for one or two correct answers, 2 marks for three or four correct answers)

b The jar containing boiling water. **(1 mark)**

c The water from the melted ice has added to the water that is already in the jar. **(1 mark)**

d It will boil and evaporate **(2 marks)**

e Condensation **(1 mark)**

f 100°C **(1 mark)**

3. a No because it has been cooked **(2 marks)**

b Irreversible change **(1 mark)**

c Melting chocolate **(1 mark)**

d (i)

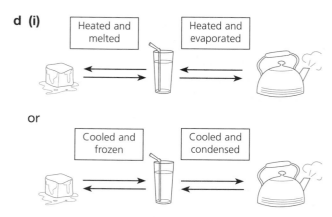

or

(3 marks: 1 mark for correct arrows, 1 mark for correct vocabulary, 1 mark for correct order)

   (ii) If the ice is heated it will melt into a liquid. If the water is heated the liquid will turn into a gas and evaporate. If the steam is cooled it will condense and turn back into water. If the water is cooled again it will freeze and turn into ice. **(2 marks)**

Physics Test 1

1. a Grain of sand – Moon
   Exercise ball – Sun
   Tennis ball – Earth **(1 mark)**

  b Any one from: every 28 days; every month; every four weeks **(1 mark)**

2. a (i)

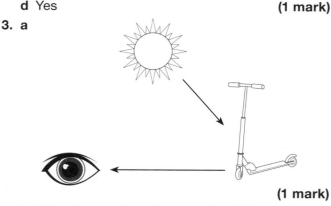

                        (1 mark)

   (ii) Yes **(1 mark)**

  b No **(1 mark)**

  c No **(1 mark)**

  d Yes **(1 mark)**

3. a

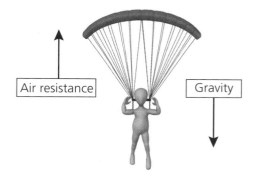

                        (1 mark)

  b Natural – one from Sun, candle, oil burner, fire
   Unnatural – one from electric light, television **(2 marks)**

4. a Long grass, carpet, tiles **(1 mark)**

  b Eventually the car will stop on all the surfaces because of friction. Friction is caused when two surfaces slide across each other. **(2 marks)**

5. a

Magnetic	Not magnetic
steel	gold
iron	copper
	plastic
	wood

(2 marks: 1 mark for each correct column)

  b The magnets will not be attracted to each other because the two north ends are facing each other. The north end needs to face the south end to attract. **(2 marks)**

  c Repel **(1 mark)**

6. a The sound is made through vibrations **(1 mark)**

  b higher
   lower **(1 mark)**

  c A soft sound is created by plucking gently on the guitar string. **(1 mark)**
   A louder sound is made by plucking the guitar string harder. **(1 mark)**

Physics Test 2

1. a

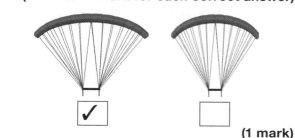

(2 marks: 1 mark for each correct arrow)

  b Air resistance – makes the parachute slow down
   Gravity – pulls the parachute to the ground/pulls the parachute towards the Earth

(2 marks: 1 mark for each correct answer)

  c

                        (1 mark)

  d The parachute on the left has a greater surface area, so the air resistance is greater for this parachute. **(2 marks)**

e The screwed up piece of paper will hit the floor first. It has less surface area than the flat piece of paper. **(2 marks)**

2. a Pulley system **(1 mark)**
 b Lever system **(1 mark)**
 c Gears consist of a system of *cogs* that allows a *small* turning force to have a *great* effect. **(3 marks)**

3. a It will increase in length. **(1 mark)**
 b

(1 mark)

4. a Venus, Jupiter, Saturn, Neptune
(2 marks: 1 mark for one to three correct answers, 2 marks for four correct answers)
 b The Sun **(1 mark)**

5. a

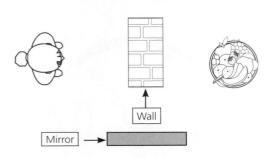

Mirror can be shown in either position. **(1 mark)**
 b A mirror reflects light, meaning the image of the bowl of fruit will reflect in the mirror and Ruby can see it. **(1 mark)**

Physics Test 3

1. a 3. The Earth must orbit the Sun! **(1 mark)**
 b The Earth rotates on its axis. When the place you are at is facing the Sun, it is light. When the place you are at is facing away from the Sun, it is dark. **(2 marks)**
 c

(1 mark)

d The Earth rotates on its axis. T
 It takes the Earth a month to orbit the Sun. F
 The Moon's full cycle is around 28 days. T
 One full rotation of the Earth takes a week. F

(3 marks: 1 mark for one or two correct answers, 2 marks for three correct answers, 3 marks for four correct answers)

2. a (i) Will work **(1 mark)**
   (ii) Will not work **(1 mark)**
 b Conductor – a material that will let an electrical current through.
 Insulator – a material that will not let an electrical current through.
 (2 marks: 1 mark for each correct answer)

c

Runs on electricity	Does not run on electricity
toaster	coal fire
lamp	gas hob
television	

(2 marks: 1 mark for each correct column)

3. a Any two from: length of the spinner's wings; width of the spinner's wings; material used to make the spinner; any other sensible change
 (2 marks: 1 mark for each change)
 b Air resistance
 Gravity
 (2 marks: 1 mark for each correct answer)
 c Dropping the spinners three times and taking an average improves the accuracy of the test. **(1 mark)**
 d

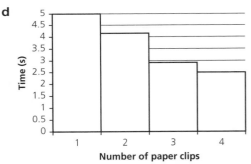

(3 marks: 1 mark for one or two correct answers, 2 marks for three correct answers, 3 marks for four correct answers)

 e The one with one paper clip. **(1 mark)**
 f As there are no paper clips on the spinner, it will fall more slowly than the spinners that have paper clips on because there is less weight. **(1 mark)**

Progress Report

Fill in your total marks for each completed test.

Colour the stars to show how you feel after completing each test.

☆ = needs practice   ☆☆ = nearly there   ☆☆☆ = got it!

Biology

Test	Marks	How do you feel?
Test 1	/ 25	☆ ☆ ☆
Test 2	/ 23	☆ ☆ ☆
Test 3	/ 25	☆ ☆ ☆

Chemistry

Test	Marks	How do you feel?
Test 1	/ 24	☆ ☆ ☆
Test 2	/ 25	☆ ☆ ☆
Test 3	/ 26	☆ ☆ ☆

Physics

Test	Marks	How do you feel?
Test 1	/ 22	☆ ☆ ☆
Test 2	/ 21	☆ ☆ ☆
Test 3	/ 23	☆ ☆ ☆